PRACTICAL TECHNIQUES

for

ENHANCING SELF-ESTEEM

Activity Book
for
Leaders and Participants

Accompanies the Book, *Enhancing Self Esteem*, 2nd ed.

Diane Frey, Ph.D.
Professor of Counseling
Wright State University
Dayton, Ohio

C. Jesse Carlock, Ph.D.
Psychologist in Private Practice
Dayton, Ohio

 ACCELERATED DEVELOPMENT
A member of the Taylor & Francis Group

Practical Techniques for Enhancing Self-Esteem

4 5 6 7 8 9 0 MGMG 9 0 9 8 7

Printed in the United States of America

Technical Development: Tanya Benn
                         Delores Kellogg
                         Marguerite Mader
                         Sheila Sheward

Cover Graphics: David Loop

Library of Congress Cataloging-in-Publication Data

Frey, Diane.
    Practical techniques for enhancing self esteem / Diane Frey, C. Jesse Carlock. -- 2nd ed.
        p.   cm.
    "A companion book to Enhancing self esteem."
    Includes bibliographical references.
    ISBN 1-55959-009-2
    1. Self-respect.   2. Self-respect--Problems, exercises, etc.
    I. Carlock, C. Jesse.   II. Frey, Diane.   Enhancing self esteem.
    III. Title.
    BF697.5.S46F75   1991
    158'.1--dc20   89-81014
                                                         CIP

LCN: 89-81014

ISBN: 1-55959-009-2

For additional information and ordering, please contact:

ACCELERATED DEVELOPMENT
A member of the Taylor & Francis Group
1900 Frost Road; Suite 101
Bristol, PA 19007
1-800-821-8312

DEDICATION

This book is dedicated with fond memory to Dr. Arthur Atkinson whose life exemplified many of the characteristics of high self-esteem.

D.F.

I dedicate this book to Kerry Glaus and my family of friends who continue to help me to love myself and to spread that love to those around me . . .

C.J.C.

TABLE OF CONTENTS

INTRODUCTION FOR THE HELPING PROFESSIONAL

The greatest gift you can ever give is the activation of the potential for positive self-esteem. This workbook is designed to help you to pass the gift of high self-esteem to others and/or yourself.

The techniques used in this workbook were developed to be a natural outgrowth of the text, *Enhancing Self Esteem* by Frey and Carlock. Frequently a technique will indicate page references from this text. Please refer to these pages to help you to understand the techniques as they interface with the theory of self-esteem.

The workbook design helps participants to record their personal comments and review them from time to time. The actual writing of responses utilizes all three learning modalities (visual, auditory, and kinesthetic), thus making the learning very powerful and memorable.

This activity book can be easily used by a group leader. The exchange of ideas in a group helps participants to learn from one another. The process of sharing and giving feedback helps one to become more self aware, thus enhancing self-esteem.

The workbook is also formatted to be used individually. A helping professional could guide a person through the workbook or an individual could use the workbook as a self help guide. The authors' have used the techniques in group and individual counseling as well as in classroom and business settings. Many people report using the techniques by themselves to increase self growth.

Most importantly and most uniquely, *Practical Techniques for Enhancing Self-Esteem* is divided into phases of intervention. The goal of these phases is to help individuals to develop positive self-esteem in a systematic, sequential approach. This stepwise progression to enhancing self-esteem is unique in the field of self-esteem. It represents the result of extensive review of the self-esteem literature, over twenty years of private practice experience for each of the authors and twenty years of graduate school teaching. The four phases are entitled (1) identity, (2) strengths and weaknesses, (3) nuturance, and (4) maintenance. Each phase is progressive and, as such, built on the other. It has been found that this four phase method of enhancing self-esteem is superior to randomly choosing activities to enhance self-esteem.

Phases

Identity Phase. Research on self-esteem indicates that individuals of low self-esteem are lacking in self awareness. It is necessary, therefore, that they develop their own identity. This identity serves as a foundation for the further development of self-esteem. Self-concept development is a major form of this phase. Techniques in this phase help individuals to introspect and become more aware of who they are.

Strengths and Weaknesses Phase. Once individuals develop their own identity, they can begin to understand their own pattern of strengths and weaknesses. This phase includes techniques to help individuals identify attributes and areas of self which represent opportunities for improvement.

Nurturance Phase. The nurturance phase of enhancing self-esteem is much like the fertilizer used to help plants develop fully. Since self-esteem is not a static concept, i.e., once established, always the same, the nurturance phase is important in that it helps individuals understand how to broaden their perspective on their own self-esteem and enrich it. Techniques in this phase focus on the development of a social support system, learning how to filter feedback from the environment, and managing self-talk.

Maintenance Phase. The maintenance phase of enhancing self-esteem builds on the other phases by helping individuals secure positive self-esteem over time. Activities in this phase focus on goal setting, risk taking, and personal forecasting.

Each technique has write-in space for the participant. Each activity also provides specific reference to the book, *Enhancing Self Esteem*, which assists the leader in understanding the theory basis for the technique. In addition, a six-step model is included to assist the helping professional in developing discussion in a group or individual setting. Facilitators can use selected techniques from each phase without doing all the activities provided the techniques are used in the four part order. Since each participant has the workbook, the leader could use some techniques in a group setting and assign some techniques for "homework" for the group or individuals. Each technique also indicates the ages for which the activity is most appropriate and the time required and materials needed. The intent of all the techniques is to translate theory into practice.

PROCESS MODEL

The recommendation is that each technique be processed using the following learning model which includes six steps.

In **Step 1, Introduction,** discuss with the participant(s) the rationale for doing the technique plus the procedure to ensure that each person understands why the intervention is being used and how it is to be done.

In **Step 2, Participation,** each person responds to the directions. Be sure to allow for some participants to not respond if the material is too threatening to them. On the other hand, a helpful procedure is for the facilitator to mention that individuals usually only benefit from an activity to the degree to which they participate.

In **Step 3, Publishing,** participants agree to share their reactions and observations about what others said. With young children a helpful procedure

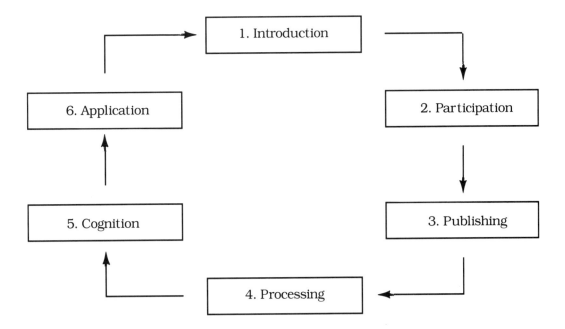

often is to ask them to review or memorize what other children have said to facilitate active listening.

In **Step 4, Processing,** participants are asked to discuss various patterns and dynamics they noticed from the participation step. The focus could be on what was similar about the responses or what was different about the responses. Be careful to avoid value judgment or evaluation of sharing.

In **Step 5, Cognition,** participants are asked to think about principles, hypotheses, and generalizations which can be developed from the activity.

In **Step 6, Application,** individuals need to recognize the relevance of the learning to their everyday life. Of course, when participants modify their behavior they begin the cycle again with a rationale for new behavior and a new experience.

If participants seem to have a difficult time responding to an intervention, consider the following continua as they relate to human interaction:

Generally people would rather talk about others than themselves;

others _____ self

Most people prefer to discuss there and then issues rather than issues of here and now;

there/then _____ here/now

Most individuals would rather discuss thought than feeling;

thought _____ feeling

And, when discussing feelings, most people would rather discuss positive feelings than negative feelings.

positive feelings _____ negative feelings

Imagine where each participant is functioning on each continuum. Try to meet the individual at the readiness point on each continuum. When helping a person to self disclose, move across the contiuum in small intervals to the right from where the person was on each continuum. Increased openness will then occur. This openness helps to increase the open area of the Johari Window, as discussed in Chapter 2 of the book, *Enhancing Self Esteem*. A large open pane of the person's window enlarges self-concept and self-awareness. Thus helping to make for a more fully functioning person.

INTRODUCTION FOR THE PARTICIPANT

This workbook is written so that you can use it in a group or individually. The techniques are included in a definite order. Be sure to follow the order of the phases, unless your leader decides to skip some techniques.

Each technique tells what materials you will need and how much time it will take. Under the purpose area, you are given the reason for doing the activity.

A helpful procedure is to talk about ideas you are learning about with friends or relatives. Sometimes you might not be able to do an activity all by yourself. If so, go to another technique in the same phase or find someone whom you trust to do this with you.

Your leader will need to refer to the textbook, *Enhancing Self Esteem*. This is meant to give background information. You do not need to refer to the textbook. When you have completed your workbook, keep it in a special place. You will find it very useful as a reference in the future. You will be able to see easily how much you are growing in self-esteem.

INTRODUCTORY TECHNIQUES FOR
THE HELPING PROFESSIONAL

Note to Leader: Read Chapter 1 of *Enhancing Self Esteem* before doing this activity.

Comments and Thoughts

"Of all the judgment we pass, none is as important as the one we pass on ourselves" (Branden, 1986). Do you agree? What psychological difficulties might be related to low self-esteem? Consider the problems of anxiety, depression, fear of intimacy, fear of failure and success, chemical dependency, underachievement, child or spousal abuse, sexual immaturity, emotional immaturity, and suicide. How might low self-esteem be related to these problems? In what other ways does self-esteem affect one's life? Take some time to write your impressions about these questions.

_____

_____

_____

_____

_____

_____

_____

_____

_____

_____

_____

_____

_____

_____

_____

_____

_____

Have you ever known anyone with no positive self-esteem or no positive self-estimates? Is it possible to have all positive self-estimates? No one is entirely lacking in positive self-esteem, nor is anyone capable of having all positive self-estimates. What are your positive self-estimates? What are some self-estimates you could improve? Take time to list some of these areas.

1. _____
2. _____
3. _____
4. _____
5. _____
6. _____

Positive self-esteem is, "state of one who is not at war either with himself or with others" (Branden, 1986). Have you felt like this? Do you know people who seem to manifest this trait? What contributes to that feeling? Record your thoughts about this below.

_____
_____
_____
_____
_____
_____
_____
_____
_____
_____
_____
_____

As you use this workbook, think about your self-esteem. Parents of high self-esteem tend to rear children of high self-esteem. Parents of low self-esteem tend to parent children of low self-esteem. Teachers of high self-esteem tend to raise the self-esteem of the students in their classroom. Teachers of low self-esteem have a negative impact on the self-esteem of their students. Your self-esteem level will be reflected in the interaction you have with others. As you help others to improve self-esteem you could be helping yourself also.

Reference

Branden, N. (1986). *How to raise your self-esteem.* New York: Bantam Books.

PART I

IDENTITY PHASE

Helping Professional

Techniques in this phase focus primarily on helping a person to discover his or her own identity. Because of the distorted perceptions people of low self-esteem often have, they rarely have a clear understanding of who they really are. Usually such individuals do not see their whole self but focus on small aspects of self. The following techniques aid in increasing individuals' awareness of their own identity.

Participants

In this phase you will learn more about who you are. You will become more aware of different aspects of yourself.

ACTIVITY 1.1
SELF-ESTEEM BANNER

Note To The Leader

The leader/teacher is to review Chapter 1 and the section on the Johari Window in the book *Enhancing Self Esteem*.

Purpose

To help acquaint individuals with the various aspects of self, i.e., ideal self, real self, fantasy self.

Time Required

45 minutes

Participants

Children and adults ages eight and over in a group or individual setting

Materials Needed

Banner sheets, pencil or pens

Procedure

1. Recognize the concept of self-esteem banners and how banners have been used for centuries to symbolize and announce who a person was (for example, a lion in a banner meant strength; a fleur-de-lis symbolized the royal family of France; a cross meant defense of Christianity).

2. On the "Self-Esteem Banner" on page 13, write or draw responses in the nine areas.

   a. In area number 1 write or draw how you would like to be, your "ideal self."
   b. In area 2 write or show what symbolizes the "real self."
   c. In area 3 picture or write what represents your "fantasy self."
   d. In area 4 put a representation of the "me" everybody knows, the "open self."
   e. In area 5 draw or write about the "me" hardly anyone knows, the "hidden self."
   f. In area 6 symbolize the unstable self-estimates you have (refer to Chapter 1 again for further clarification).
   g. In area 7 tell about the things you do well, your "present self."
   h. In area 8 represent the things you would like to do well, your "self in process."
   i. In area 9 write or symbolize one thing you would like to have said of you if you died today.

3. After completing the Self-Esteem Banner, share your banner with group members and the facilitator by

   a. posting anonymously the banners and having group members try to match banners with individuals; or

b.   wearing your banner, circulating around in the room, and reading each other's banner.

Note: If done in a one-to-one setting, share with your teacher or significant other person in your life.

4.   After sharing in Procedure 3, answer the following:

a.   What kinds of things were shared by others with you that reinforced or confirmed your concepts of yourself?

_____

_____

_____

_____

_____

b.   What kinds of things were shared by others with you that cause you to wonder about or to see yourself a little differently?

_____

_____

_____

_____

_____

5.   Write about the area of the "self" that was easiest to represent in the Self-Esteem Banner.

_____

_____

_____

_____

_____

6.   Write about the area of the "self" that was hardest to represent in the Self-Esteem Banner.

_____

_____

_____

_____

_____

Self-Esteem Banner

8.

3.

1.   2.

4.   5.

6.

7.

9.

ACTIVITY 1.2
FORTUNE COOKIES

Purpose

To help the participant to begin to reveal aspects of self and become more familiar with the "real self."

Time Required

30 minutes

Participants

Young children to senior citizens in an individual or group setting

Material Needed

One fortune cookie for each participant

Procedure

1. Choose one fortune cookie.

2. Open the cookie and read the fortune.

3. Then discuss the content of the fortune which has more relevance for you. For example the fortune might say, "You will have a great adventure." Perhaps you believe that you are very adventurous or maybe you feel you are not adventurous. Your responses can indicate what aspects of the fortune might be true or false for you.

4. If you are doing this in a group setting, give feedback to others as they present, thus increasing self awareness. Follow the guidelines discussed in the introduction for processing this activity.

5. As you discussed the content of your fortune cookie, write what you revealed about yourself.

_____

_____

_____

6. As others give you feedback from your discussion about the content of your fortune cookie, write what they helped you reveal about yourself.

_____

_____

_____

Note: This technique was first shared with one of the authors by Dr. Keith Ward, Training Consultant, San Diego, California.

ACTIVITY 1.3
JOHARI WINDOW SANDWICHES

Note To The Leader

The leader is to review the section in *Enhancing Self Esteem* on the Johari Window and definitions of different types of selves and share with the group.

Purpose

To help individuals understand their various selves more thoroughly and to consolidate self estimates into a stable aggregate.

Time Required

Approximately 30 minutes

Participants

Any number: young children, adolescents, or adults in a group or individual setting

Materials Needed

Enough paper for two pieces for each participant, pencil or pen, masking tape

Procedure

1. Discuss the Johari Window.

2. Draw or write on a piece of paper things which indicate the open part of yourself.

3. On the reverse side of this paper, draw or write a description of the private aspects of your self.

4. On the other piece of paper, draw or write descriptions of some of your blind areas.

5. On the back of this piece of paper, write descriptions of what might be in the unknown self.

6. Tape the piece of paper with the open area of the Johari Window on your shoulder, covering your chest.

7. Tape the piece of paper with the blind area showing on your shoulder, covering your back. By so doing you have created a self-sandwich with the open area facing outward, the private self facing inward toward your chest, the blind area is facing outward on the back, and the unknown area is facing inward on the back.

8. Mill around and exchange information about different aspects of self. Do so as much as you can and still feel comfortable. If you want to share the private self, you may. If not, this is also acceptable.

9. If you would like to write additional comments about the blind area of others, please do so and share that with the respective person. Each participant would, therefore, learn more about their blind areas.

10. When each participant has talked with at least four others, process the activity according to the guidelines mentioned in the introduction of this workbook.

11. Answer the following questions:

    a. As you moved about as a Johari Window Sandwich, how did you feel as you recognized certain aspects of self that were showing to others, some were known by you but not showing, and others could be seen about you but were blind for you?

        _____

        _____

        _____

        _____

    b. How much of the "private self" did you share and how willingly?

        _____

        _____

        _____

        _____

    c. What things, if any, were shared by others with you about you?

        _____

        _____

        _____

        _____

    d. How are your self-estimates in relation to what others are saying to you?

        _____

        _____

        _____

        _____

Variations in Procedure

Ask very young children to cut and/or paste pictures on these pieces of paper which represent various aspects of self.

When this activity is done in an individual setting, the helping professional can ask the participant to complete the self-sandwich as indicated and then discuss all four sides with the helper according to the earlier mentioned process guidelines.

ACTIVITY 1.4
SELF-ESTEEM FACIAL SCULPTURES

Note To The Leader

As described in Chapter 4 of the book *Enhancing Self Esteem* in the section about self perception, often individuals are unaware of their feelings, behaviors, or thoughts. This lack of awareness causes one to minimize the open area of self as described in Chapter 1. Individuals low in self-esteem often lack self-awareness. (The leader is to review the symptoms of low self-esteem in Chapter 6)

Purpose

To develop more self-awareness of feelings.

Time Required

30 minutes

Participants

Any number in a group setting; children, adolescents or adults

Material Needed

None (mirrors could be used)

Procedure

1. Find another person with whom you would like to work.

2. One of you, sculpt the other's face to represent a feeling.

3. After completing Procedure 2, have the rest of the group to guess what feeling this facial expression reveals (another way of doing this is to ask the participant whose face has been sculpted to look in a mirror and guess what feeling this is).

4. Take turns in sculpting the feelings of, for example, happiness, anger, sorrow, grief, confusion, embarrassment, loneliness, surprise.

5. Answer the following questions:

   a. As others guessed what feeling was revealed about you (Procedure 3), how did their comments "fit" with your own concepts?

   _____

   _____

   _____

   _____

b. Based on what happened in this activity, how well do you perceive yourself showing your feelings?

_____

_____

_____

_____

c. What things occurred during the activity that helped you reach the answer given to 5b?

_____

_____

_____

_____

NOTE: An important learning from this technique is that people of high self-esteem have all these feelings as do people of low self-esteem. How one copes with these feelings is what often differentiates high self-esteem individuals from low self-esteem individuals. The leader is to review Chapter 4 for much more information on this topic.

ACTIVITY 1.5
UNDERSTANDING THE CHILD-SELF

Note To The Leader

As discussed in Chapter 2, *Enhancing Self Esteem,* numerous factors influence the development of self-concept and self-esteem. One of these is the child-self, the child-self within all adults. Everyone has a self-estimate called the child-self which represents aspects of the child we once were. The child-self is welcomed and integrated by those of high self-esteem. The child-self is discounted and often repudiated by those of low self-esteem. When one is aware of the child-self, spontaneity and playfulness result. Not understanding that child-self often leads to inappropriate adult behavior and low self-esteem.

Branden (1987) suggests the following technique for understanding the child-self.

Purpose

To assist one in understanding the child-self.

Time Required

30 to 60 minutes

Participants

Teenagers and adults in individual or group settings

Materials Needed

Photograph(s) of self as a child, paper, pencils

Procedure

1. Find a photograph of yourself as a child.

2. Spend a few minutes looking at this child-self.

3. Close your eyes and relax, and ask yourself these questions: a. What was it like to be five years old? b. What was it like living in your home? c. How did you feel?

4. Open your eyes and complete these sentence stems working as rapidly as possible, avoiding censoring.

    a. When I was five years old . . . _____

    _____

    _____

b. When I was ten years old . . . _____

_____

_____

c. If the child in me could respond, she/he might say . . . _____

_____

_____

d. One of the things I had to do as a child was _____

_____

_____

e. One of the ways I treat my child-self or my mother (father) did
is _____

_____

_____

f. When I look at myself from this perspective . . . _____

_____

_____

5. Do this activity several times at different intervals of about a month apart. Avoid looking at prior sentence endings before completing the stems again. Each occasion will bring new insights about self-esteem.

Variation in Procedure

A variation of this technique is to focus on the teenage-self. This activity is one for adults. The participants could focus on a picture of self as a teenager. Then complete the same sentence stem, substituting teenage for child in the stems already listed. Both techniques help one to accept the child-self and the teenage-self inside oneself.

Reference

Branden, Nathaniel (1987). *How to Raise your Self Esteem.* New York: Bantam Books.

ACTIVITY 1.6
RETRO MACHINE

Purpose

To begin to nurture the child-self or teenage-self within.

Time Required

30 minutes or more

Participants

Adolescents or adults in individual or group settings

Materials Needed

Paper and pencil or pen

Procedure

1. Review your responses to the activity, Understanding the Child-Self or Understanding the Teenage-Self in Activity 1.5.

2. Close your eyes and imagine you are in a time machine. You can go back to any time in your life in this retro machine. Go back to a time during which you feel you needed more nurturing.

3. Imagine seeing yourself at this age. Dialogue with your child-self. Ask this child-self what it wants.

4. Imagine holding the child-self in your lap. Tell the child-self what it wants to hear. Continue to nurture this child-self.

5. Open your eyes when you have completed this activity.

6. In the space provided, write what you said to the child-self.

7. Ask a friend to tell you these things or make it a goal to tell yourself these things, thus developing yourself as your own best friend. For example, perhaps your child-self said accept me unconditionally, be there for me, rock me. A friend would say to you, "I'll always be there for you." "I accept you as you are." You could rock yourself or a friend could rock you while telling you this.

_____

_____

_____

_____

8. Answer the following:

a. How do you feel as you or a friend tells you the things you identified in Procedure 6?

_____

_____

_____

_____

b. All of us need nurturing. What are your major nurturing needs?

_____

_____

_____

_____

Variation in Procedure

For adults, a continuation of this technique would be to do it for the teenage-self.

ACTIVITY 1.7
SELF-ESTEEM METAPHORS

Note To The Leader

This method is for self-awareness and learning more about self through projection. This technique helps participants to discover more about their identity. Self for others is self-estimate discussed in Chapter 2. The leader is to review that section before doing this technique.

Purpose

To help participants to discover more about their identity.

Time Required

20 to 30 minutes

Participants

Young children or adults in a group setting

Material Needed

None

Procedure

1. Choose a metaphor you would like to be described as, i.e., a book, a pet, a piece of furniture, a tree, or musical instrument.

2. Write what you chose in Procedure 1. _____

3. As other participants identify the metaphor they chose, tell each what type of book, for example, you experience the person as. The book might be *Pilgrim's Progress,* the *Bible, Adventures With Charlie,* etc. Also tell the person the reason for your choice.

4. After you have received input from other participants you chose, answer the following:

   a. As other participants shared what type of metaphor you were and their reasons for those choices, how well did their comments agree with your concepts and why?

   _____

   _____

   b. Based on responses you received from others, summarize the kind of identity you believe you have in the "eyes" of others.

   _____

   _____

Variation in Procedure

This technique also can be developed to include not only what metaphor would one want to choose, but also what metaphor would one not want to choose. Discuss the reasons behind the choices.

ACTIVITY 1.8
SELF COMPASSION

Background

Often people are much more compassionate to others than they are to themselves.

Purpose

To help you give yourself more compassion.

Time Required

30 minutes

Participants

Children age eight or over, adolescents, and adults; individual or group settings

Procedure

1. Think about what you say to yourself when you are very self-critical.

2. Engage in that dialogue silently for awhile.

3. Imagine a friend coming to you and telling you that he or she says these same things to herself or himself.

4. Think of what you would tell this person who engaged in real self-criticism.

5. Tell yourself the same advice.

6. Record what advice you gave to yourself.

   _____

   _____

7. Share how you could be more self compassionate.

   _____

   _____

Note to Leader: Please review Chapter 4, in the book, *Enhancing Self Esteem*, on internal dynamics of self and the activity in Chapter 6, "Managing the Pig." This is a helpful corollary activity to this one.

ACTIVITY 1.9
SELF-ESTEEM BINGO

Purpose

To help develop self-esteem and respect for others by giving positive feedback in a game format.

Time Required

30 to 60 minutes

Participants

Children age eight and over, adolescents, and adults. This is a group activity.

Materials Needed

1. One Bingo sheet should be made for each person in the group.

2. Different numbers have to be put in each block, and each Bingo sheet should have numbers arranged differently. Under the E the blocks may have numbers from 1 through 15; under S, numbers from 16 through 30; under T, numbers from 31 through 45; under EE, numbers from 46 through 60; and under M, numbers 61 through 75. Example: Under the "E" column you might have 2, 14, 7, 10, and 5 on one card and 14, 10, 7, 6, and 2 on another card, etc.

3. The leader will need a master set of numbers from which to draw. Cut paper squares, numbered 1 to 75.

4. Each person will need approximately 20 markers to use when covering his/her blocks. Cut squares from construction paper or use paper clips, buttons, or other small objects.

Procedure

1. If the number of participants is large, divide into smaller groups of 10 to 15 participants in each group.

2. Draw a number from a box containing the 75 squares with numbers.

3. Choose one or rotate variations of having members openly participate.

    a. Pick a number and have each person with that number share his/ her square. Continue until someone gets a line and calls out "Esteem." This method takes the most time.

    b. Pick an Esteem number and only periodically have the participants share their square. Example: "The next number I pick is a pass for everyone. Mark the square but don't share it." Then, "The next number I pick will be to share." Continue until someone has Esteem.

    c.   Go around the circle within each group, if you have more than one group, starting with the first 2 participants. Pick a number and if they have it, they share. Go on to the next 2 participants, etc. Meanwhile everyone fills the cards until someone calls Esteem.

    d.   Pick the numbers and periodically share until someone has Esteem.

    e.   Pick a number and say "Anyone who has the number in this row will share," etc.

    f.   When someone gets Esteem, he or she stands up and say "I Am a Worthy Person" and share all 5 of the squares.

4.   If desired to do so, award suitable prizes.

5.   Have a closing discussion.

    a.   What are some things we liked about this game?

    b.   What are some things we didn't like about this game?

6.   Complete the following:

    a.   What positive things did you see others in the group gain?

    _____

    b.   How did you feel about giving positive feedback to others during the game?

    _____

    _____

    c.   If you received positive feedback from others during the game, what was that positive feedback?

    _____

    d.   What positive things did you gain about yourself as a result of playing the game?

    _____

    _____

SELF-ESTEEM BINGO

E	S	T	EE	M
Name a person you respect.	Tell something you are proud you can do	Name two things you look for in a friend	Tell one way you are different and one way you are the same as others	Give a positive compliment to someone
Tell one thing you could teach someone else	Say something nice about the person of your choice	Name a time a friend helped you out	Name a famous person you'd like to meet	Say one thing you like about yourself
Name two people who are important to you	Tell one way you put yourself down	**FREE**	Give a compliment to someone	Tell one thing you like about your class
Say one quality of friendship that you have	Tell one thing you <u>like</u> and one thing you <u>dislike</u> about this activity	Name something you like about your teacher and tell him/her	Tell what you would do with $100.00	Your advice to the world would be ...
Name something you've learned about self esteem.	Say what you like best about your family	Give a compliment to the person whose birthday is closest to yours	Tell about a time you helped out a friend	Tell two things that make you smile

ACTIVITY 1.10
HOWITZER MANTRAS

Note To The Leader

The internal self critic often leads one into low self-esteem and perpetuates low self-esteem. The Howitzer Mantras as described by McKoy and Fanning (1987) are selected words and phrases designed to help overcome this.

Purpose

To disarm negative self talk.

Time Required

5 to 10 minutes

Participants

Any number; young children to adults; individual or group setting

Materials Needed

None

Procedure

1. Begin to think negative self thought(s) such as, "I'm really stupid," or "I can't do anything right."

2. While thinking the negative self thoughts, choose one of the following mantras to say to yourself:

    > This is poison! Stop it!
    > These are lies.
    > These are lies my father (mother, brother, sister, etc.) told me.
    > No more put-downs.
    > Shut up!
    > Get off my back! Stop this garbage!

3. Shout these Howitzer Mantras inside yourself. Mentally swear at the self-critic.

4. Stop the self thoughts and record some of your feelings

    a. When you started your negative self thoughts, how did you feel?

    _____

    _____

    _____

    _____

b.　　As you started saying the Howitzer Mantras to yourself, how did your feelings change?

_____

_____

_____

_____

c.　　What changes, if any, did you notice as you started shouting the Howitzer Mantras to yourself?

_____

_____

_____

_____

Variation in Procedure

For an additional strong method, participants can be encouraged to put a rubber band around their wrist and snap it while subvocalizing the mantra. By snapping the rubber band participants emphasize the "stop" command and make thought interruption more likely.

Reference

McKoy, M., & Fanning, P. (1987). *Self-Esteem.* Oakland, CA: New Harbinger Publications.

ACTIVITY 1.11
SELF-ESTEEM SENTENCE COMPLETION

Note To The Leader

Characteristic of individuals with low self-esteem is a lack of self-awareness. The following sentence items are taken from Branden's (1986) sentence completion technique. By revealing one's innermost self for the completion of these sentences, more self awareness evolves.

Purpose

To increase self awareness.

Time Required

45 minutes

Participants

Any number, adolescents or adults

Materials Needed

Paper and pen

Procedure

1. Find a quiet place and write as many responses as you can (between 6-8) to each sentence item. Work rapidly and do not censor yourself.

    a. I like myself most when I. . . _____

        _____

        _____

        _____

    b. I like myself least when. . . _____

        _____

        _____

        _____

    c. Mother gave me a view of myself as . . . _____

        _____

        _____

        _____

    d. Father gave me a view of myself as . . . _____

        _____

        _____

        _____

e.　When I feel disliked. . .　_____

_____

_____

_____

f.　If I look at the criteria by which I judge myself . . .　_____

_____

_____

_____

g.　If no one can give me a good self-esteem except myself . . .　_____

_____

_____

_____

h.　One of the things I can do to raise my self-esteem is . . .　_____

_____

_____

_____

i.　As I learn to accept myself . . .　_____

_____

_____

_____

j.　If I were willing to see what I see right now . . .　_____

_____

_____

_____

k.　I am becoming aware . . .　_____

_____

_____

_____

l.　As I become more willing to understand what I am writing . . .　_____

_____

_____

_____

2. When you have completed the sentence items in Procedure 1, focus on what you have learned about yourself. Summarize those learnings in the space provided.

_____

_____

_____

_____

_____

_____

3. If you are in a group setting, share your responses with others.

4. Ask for feedback about what others are learning about your identity. Summarize their comments.

_____

_____

_____

_____

_____

_____

5. Give feedback to others about things you notice in their responses.

Reference

Branden, N. (1986). *How to raise your self-esteem.* New York: Bantam Books.

ACTIVITY 1.12
NEWSPAPER IDENTITY

Note To The Leader

On pages 3 through 12 in *Enhancing Self Esteem,* several different aspects of self are discussed. As discussed in *Enhancing Self Esteem,* knowledge of self-estimates is very important for everyone who is trying to improve self-esteem. The more knowledgeable one is about various self-estimates, the larger the OPEN area of the Johari Window. (The leader should review pages 3 through 7 in the book.)

Purpose

To develop a better understanding of your identity.

Time Required

25 to 30 minutes

Participants

Students in grades 4 through 12 and adults in individual or group setting

Materials Needed

Several old newspapers, rolls of tape, and/or glue stick. For each participant a sheet of newsprint and a pair of scissors.

Procedure

1. Compose a brief autobiographical sketch of self using words, phrases or sentences from newspapers.

2. Contribute phrases to each other if you know one another well enough at the time this activity is done.

3. Cut and paste on newsprint several (at least five) words, phrases, or sentences which describe yourself.

4. When everyone is finished, share autobiographical sheets. (These sheets will reveal various self-estimates.)

5. Answer the following:

    a. What kinds of words, phrases, and/or sentences were contributed to you by other participants?

    _____

    _____

    _____

    _____

b. How did the words help you gain new insight into yourself if they did?

_____

_____

_____

_____

c. Were the words, phrases, and/or sentences that were contributed by others fairly well in agreement or were they quite different?

_____

_____

_____

_____

d. If they were very much alike, what did that tell you?

_____

_____

_____

_____

e. If they were quite different, what did that tell you?

_____

_____

_____

_____

Variation in Procedure

When working individually with another, the facilitator could assign this as a "homework" between sessions or ask the person to complete this task during the session.

PART II

STRENGTHS AND WEAKNESSES PHASE

Helping Professional

Techniques in the strengths and weaknesses phase help individuals expand upon the awareness they have acquired from the identity phase to discover which areas of self are strengths and which are weaknesses. This phase helps individuals surface aspects of self for which they have had little awareness. In this phase is where they really evaluate these aspects of self and become more aware of a variegation of strengths and weaknesses. In this phase individuals learn a valid process of evaluating patterns of strengths and weaknesses within the self.

Participant

In this section of the workbook you will learn more about what you like about yourself and what you do not like about yourself. You will become more aware of how your strengths can help to strengthen your weaknesses.

ACTIVITY 2.1
THE GIFT

Note To The Leader

In Chapter 1 of *Enhancing Self Esteem*, the Johari Window is discussed. In the blind and unknown quadrant are positive qualities of oneself which have not as yet been owned. These positive qualities are frequently projected outside of the person (see discussion on projection, Chapters 3 and 4). By discovering such unclaimed parts, one can fill in missing pieces of self-concept. Identifying strengths as well as weaknesses is crucial for self-esteem enhancement.

Purposes

1. To identify positive aspects of oneself that may as yet be unowned or not fully integrated.

2. To support the absorption of positive self-attributes to create a warmer feeling about self.

Time Required

   30 minutes

Participants

   8-year old or older

Materials Needed

   Pen, crayons or colored markers

Note

   If working alone, have someone else read the procedure to you or use a tape recorder to record the directions and then play the tape recorded directions. Either of these methods will enable you to relax and more fully participate.

Procedure

1. Allow your eyes to close and then focus your attention on your breathing.

2. Be sure your feet are flat on the floor.

3. Follow your breath as it moves in and out.

4. With each exhalation, move deeper and deeper into a feeling of peace and relaxation.

5. When you are relaxed, imagine a gift box before you.

      a.   What size it it?
      b.   How is it wrapped?
      c.   What is the box made of?

6. Now, give yourself permission to open the gift.

      a.   Notice how you feel as you do this.
      b.   What do you find inside?
      c.   Study the gift very carefully, noting each of it's qualities—age, shape, weight, texture, color—notice everything about it.
      d.   Where did it come from?
      e.   What is it used for?

7. Try to identify with this object.

8. As this object, describe yourself, your qualities, your existence, your purpose.

9. Now think of yourself and list your qualities that are similar to those of the gift.

    _____

    _____

    _____

10. Identify with the gift and write a description of yourself as the object.

    _____

    _____

    _____

11. Draw a picture of the gift.

12. Read your description and show your picture to your partner/group.

ACTIVITY 2.2
GROUP PRAISE

Purposes

1. To help participants in giving recognition and praise to others.

2. To assist in becoming more aware of one's responses to recognition from others.

Time Required

40 minutes

Participants

Children (age eight or older) or adults in a group setting of no more than twenty participants

Materials Needed

Blank paper and a pencil for each participant

Procedure

1. Compose a list of

   a. three things I do well. _____

   _____

   _____

   b. a recent success or accomplishment. _____

   _____

   _____

   c. a brief statement about what I would like to have said about me.

   _____

   _____

   _____

2. Obtain a blank piece of paper and a writing instrument (pen or pencil).

3. Pair off and exchange with your partner the information recorded in Item 1.

4. Compose a letter of recognition for your partner based on the information exchanged. This letter is written directly to the partner, not a third party.

5. When finished with Item 4, exchange letters and reflect on its content without talking.

6. Reconvene the larger group.

7. Have each person introduce his/her partner, while standing beside the person (the person being introduced does not comment at this time). The basis of the introduction is information from Items 1 and 4.

8. After all members are introduced, provide participants with an opportunity to clarify any information given about himself or herself.

9. Reflect on how you presented your partner and what you might have said about him or her (i.e., what value of yours was evident in the presentation of your partner?).

10. Reflect on what you learned about yourself. Was it easier to give the feedback or receive the feedback?

ACTIVITY 2.3
FAMILY RULES

Note To The Leader

Re-read pages 68-70 in the book *Enhancing Self Esteem*, on family rules before moving to this activity.

Background Information

Family rules are stated and reinforced both implicitly and explicitly. An important procedure within the family and for an individual is to examine these rules and update them regularly. Many times we carried such rules from our family of origin, never having updated them for ourselves, and continue to pass them along to our current families. While a family cannot effectively operate without some guiding rules, overly rigid or outdated rules can be a hindrance to healthy development.

Purposes

1. To guide participants in surfacing and evaluating a variety of family rules which were conveyed either indirectly or directly in the family origin. Often people are not aware of rules they have ingested which continue to govern their behavior. Just as often, they have never evaluated the rules to see if they are still useful.

2. To provide participants with the opportunity to revise such rules so that they are more fitting with current needs and values.

Time Required

30 minutes

Participants

Adolescents and adults

Materials Needed

Pen or pencil

Procedure

1. Record your family rules (explicit and implicit) under the categories listed below. Rules involve "Dos and Don'ts", "Shoulds and Shouldn'ts." Invite friends or family members to help you with this work.

2. Evaluate each rule and write your revision to each rule under column, "My Values."

Category	Rules From Family of Origin	My Values
Feelings		
	_____	
	_____	
	_____	
Space		
	_____	
	_____	
	_____	
Time		
	_____	
	_____	
	_____	
Money		
	_____	
	_____	
	_____	
Privacy		
	_____	
	_____	
	_____	
Secrets		
	_____	
	_____	
	_____	
Neighbors		
	_____	
	_____	
	_____	

Category	Rules From Family of Origin	My Values

Sexuality

_____

_____

_____

Play

_____

_____

_____

Touching

_____

_____

_____

Sex Rules

_____

_____

_____

Body

_____

_____

_____

Religion

_____

_____

_____

Food

_____

_____

_____

Category	Rules From Family of Origin	My Values

Others (Specify)

_____

_____

_____

3. Make a note in the margin beside "Rules from Family of Origin" as to the person from whom you adopted each rule.

4. Evaluate and make any changes in any of these rules that you would like to change. Which rules do you want to change and have trouble changing?

5. Practice revising each rule to fit with current values.

Rules Requiring Change	Revision
Example: Don't touch anyone.	I can touch others with their permission and in ways which feel good to the other person and me.

_____

_____

_____

_____

6. Find someone whom you trust. Ask this person to take each of the new values you wish to integrate and ask that person to deliver to you these new messages. For example:

   "You have a right to all of your feelings."
   "It's okay to refuse to be touched."
   "You deserve to take time for yourself each day."

7. As you listen to these messages, practice soaking in these words. Ask your friend to remind you of these new messages whenever he or she thinks you need to hear them. You also can ask to hear them.

ACTIVITY 2.4
MAGIC GARDEN

Note To The Leader

In Chapter 4 in the book, *Enhancing Self Esteem*, is a discussion of how beliefs that one holds about self can cause one to wall off parts of self which might otherwise be resources (see pages 110-111). Later in Chapter 4 is a discussion of the multifaceted self. In fact, the more differentiated the self-concept, the higher the self-esteem (see page 116). The following activities help to expand awareness of strengths.

Purposes

1. To discover positive ways to see self in the moment.

2. To identify what each participant might need for self right now (areas to improve upon or to expand).

3. To help group members get to know each other better.

Time Required

30 to 60 minutes

Participants

Any age (preadolescent or older) in group setting

Materials Needed

None

Note

If working alone, have someone else read the procedure to you or use a tape recorder to record the directions and then play the tape recorded directions for yourself. Stop the recorder when and where you need time to work through the suggested activity.

Procedure

1. Say, I'd like for you to allow your eyes to close right now and pay attention to your breathing—breathing in to the count of four, holding for four counts, 1, 2, 3, 4 and exhaling slowly through your mouth and nose to the count of eight—exhaling the last bit of air from your lungs. Try this two more times and then go back to your regular breathing. Feel the air moving in, filling your chest, then feel your chest slowly fall as you exhale. With each exhalation you feel more and more relaxed, secure, at ease.

    Now imagine, if you will, that you are walking down a beautiful, peaceful country road—a road that leads to a magical garden, a place you've never visited before. You've heard many wonderful stories about this magic garden and today you have been given the chance to go there. As you walk down this peaceful road you can begin to see the gate to the garden in the distance up ahead. Be in touch with how you feel as you slowly approach the entrance ahead. It's a beautiful sunny day. Notice the flowers and trees along the way, listen for the birds, feel the gentle breeze against your skin.

As you reach the gate you pull a key from your pocket, unlock the gate and move inside, closing the gate behind you. This is your private paradise for the next few minutes. Take your time and look around. It's more beautiful than you could ever have imagined. Lush vegetation, flowers of all colors and variety, woods and streams, birds and harmless little creatures of all varieties abound. Every where you look there's something else even more exquisite to behold. It seems that *anything you wish for suddenly appears*—that's what is so magical about this place. The sky is wide and expansive with puffy pure white clouds splashed on a pale blue background. The sun illuminates and warms everything around. Butterflies and birds of every variety fly all around adding color, song, and even more life and energy to your paradise.

As you walk around find something or some place you find yourself drawn to—maybe it's a tree, flower, bird, stream, or rock — anything you find yourself attracted to. Walk around until you find that one thing which draws your attention. Take some time to study this. When you have made your choice begin identifying with it. Describe yourself as this item in the garden—for example:

> I am an old oak tree. I stand tall and have many branches which reach out and up into the sky. Animals run up and down my sturdy trunk and birds rest and build nests on my strong branches. I'm so tall I can easily get an overview of the entire garden. My roots grow deep and wide. Sometimes people lean against me and rest or read books. My leaves provide welcomed shade.

2. Pick something in the garden with which you identify. Describe yourself in the space provided. What do you have to offer?

_____

_____

_____

_____

_____

_____

3. Now continuing to imagine yourself as this time, what do you need for yourself?

For example: "As the oak tree, I need a bird to fly through my branches and add color to me."

I need _____

_____

_____

_____

_____

_____

4. Now describe yourself as this item that you need. For example:

"I am a bird—a cardinal. I'm a bright colored red bird and I love to sing and fly through the garden hopping on branches, walking through the grass, gliding through the sky. I'm light, I'm free."

Describe:

_____

_____

_____

_____

_____

5. As a group, create a garden with participants as roleplayers portraying that with which each identified. Start with one element and add parts one or two at a time. Have each participant to act out his or her part.

What do we have first?

Example: I am the sun—I am . . . (describe self).
What I need is . . . (plants).

Do we have any plants?

I'm a rose garden—I am . . .(describe self).

I'm a lilac bush—I am. . . (describe self).

As the rose garden, what do you need?

I'd like a stream.

Do we have a stream?

Yes, I'm a stream. I am . . .(describe self).

Continue until all participants are incorporated into the garden.

6. Have each participant to look around and observe what treasures others have to offer.

7. Write your identification with something in this activity that helped you see yourself?

_____

_____

_____

_____

_____

8. Review the part of the garden you identified as a need. Does this need represent a part of you that is underdeveloped? What part? Explain.

_____

_____

_____

_____

_____

ACTIVITY 2.5
THE AUTOMOBILE METAPHOR

Purposes

1. To use metaphor as one way through which to contact our strengths and weaknesses and widen our self-perception.

2. To take a look in a playful way at group roles.

Time Required

60 minutes

Participants

At least eight participants; adolescents and adults

Materials Needed

None

Procedure

1. Think of your group as an automobile. If your group was an automobile, what part of that automobile would you be?

2. Have group members, one by one, volunteer to act out different parts of the automobile until all members are in the center of the circle demonstrating the various parts.

3. Now, as this part, describe to the group members what you're made of, attach several descriptors to this part, tell what you do.

4. Think about the part you played and identify what strengths you possess.

5. Try to relate how the function of this part relates to the role you play in the group.

6. Describe what other part of the car you'd like to play. What are the qualities of this part?

_____

_____

_____

_____

_____

_____

_____

7. Identify what goals you would set for yourself in this group to develop this part.

_____

_____

_____

_____

_____

8. Think about the different roles played in the group. Would you have assigned someone in the group a different part than they chose? If so, give the person this feedback and explain why.

_____

_____

_____

_____

_____

ACTIVITY 2.6
PUT-DOWN HUNT

Note To The Leader

Review the section in Chapter 6, *Enhancing Self Esteem,* on feedback filtering, and "Managing the Pig" before proceeding with this activity.

Purpose

To identify how often, when, and how people engage in self-criticism.

Time Required

Varying, depending on how this is specifically implemented.

Participants

Preadolescents, adolescents, and adults in individual or group setting

Materials Needed

None

Procedure

1. Take time to go on a put-down hunt. Use a particular time of the day such as lunch break, recess, or of an evening.

2. Keep track of how many times people with whom you come in contact give themselves or others put-downs.

3. Repeat the process for two or three times and notice how much you become conscious of the damage of put-downs.

4. Discuss with others in your study group how, if at all, you and they have become more guarded against put-downs.

Variations in Procedure

1. Organize a certain day where you and other study group members go on a put-down hunt over an extended period of a few hours.

2. For children develop a puppet show in which the audience's task is to tally the number of put-downs portrayed.

3. Conduct a "Stroke Hunt" where you look for positive comments others give.

Note: This technique is adapted from the allegory by Sidney Simon (1977) entitled *Vulture.* Niles, IL: Argus Communication.

ACTIVITY 2.7
DIFFERENCES

Note To The Leader

People are often drawn to others who are similar, however, a support network comprised also of people who are different from us can introduce us to values, ideas, attitudes, hobbies, careers, and ways of being. Review support networks in the book *Enhancing Self Esteem*, pages 69-73, before having the participants do this activity. Complete the assessment of your network which is included there. Then, look at the adjectives you selected to describe yourself and compare them with the adjectives you chose to describe people in your support circle. Which people are most different from you?

Purposes

1. To help us recognize that people who are different from us can be some of our best teachers and can help us to expand ourselves.

2. To identify underdeveloped parts which may need strengthening.

Time Required

30 minutes

Participants

Any number; adolescents and adults

Materials Needed

Paper and pen

Procedure

1. Write the names of three people you know who are very different from you.

   _____

   _____

   _____

2. Pick one on whom to focus.

   _____

3. Imagine being that person. What would it be like?

   _____

   _____

   _____

4. Spend some time with this person. This person potentially is your best teacher for this underdeveloped aspect of you. Ask the person to tell you about the advantages of this quality.

    _____

    _____

    _____

    _____

    _____

5. Write three of your learnings.

    _____

    _____

    _____

    _____

    _____

Note: Adapted from exercise presented at Gestalt Institute of Cleveland Intensive Post Graduate Training Program, Summer, 1986.

ACTIVITY 2.8
CHALLENGING SELF-TALK

Note To The Leader

Review Chapter 4, in *Enhancing Self Esteem*, especially the section on cognitive distortion related to self-esteem.

Purposes

1. To enable you to challenge some of your cognitive distortions, especially the distortion of overgeneralizing.

2. To help you recognize how this distortion often prevents one from moving forward in life because one continues to think of self in erroneous ways.

Time Required

30 to 45 minutes

Participants

Any number; children age eight or over, adolescents or adults in individual or group settings.

Materials Needed

Paper and pencil

Procedure

1. Think of a negative self estimate or trait about yourself that you do not like and write it in the space provided.

2. Review how you conceptualized the trait. Most likely the response was one word or in a short sentence such as "I'm always late," "I never am considerate of others," or "I'm lazy."

3. Record three situations where that trait is not exhibited in your life.

4. List three situations where you have exhibited the appropriate behavior of this trait.

5. Visualize yourself doing this positive trait.

6. Visualize this positive behavior occuring three times a day.

7. Process this activity according to the earlier guidelines discussed at the beginning of this workbook. Frequently participants discover that what they thought was always true of them is not always the case.

8. Observe over a period of time to see if visualizing the one positive trait helps you to change the focus of your thoughts.

ACTIVITY 2.9
HOW NOT TO BE

Note To The Leader

In Chapter 2, *Enhancing Self Esteem*, the major sources from which one develops a view of self are reviewed. One source is from feedback from others. In Chapter 4, introjects about self are discussed. Many times certain inner resources were not fully developed since they were not valued by our caregivers. We may have even been actively discouraged from developing particular traits if such characteristics did not fit with the family value system.

Purpose

To recognize how to be loved and accepted we often learned to cut off or reject parts of ourselves.

Time Required

20 minutes

Participants

Any number; adolescents and adults

Materials Needed

Pen

Procedure

1. Recall when you were a kid and what the rules were that you had to follow. What were the things you should be in order to be accepted, loved? What were the don't be's as well?

    Examples:

    Be polite.
    Be good.
    Don't say what you feel—you might hurt someone.
    Don't ask questions (you'll look stupid).
    Don't stare.
    Don't touch.

2. Make a list of these "rules."

    _____

    _____

    _____

    All the "don't be's" make us come from a place of fear. We learn a highly developed skill in how not to be.

3. Recall what, as a child, you probably were told about being too much of some things or not enough of some things. Make a list of these:

Too Much	**Not Enough**
Too fat	Not aggressive enough
Too tall	Not talkative enough
Too short	Not neat enough
Too sloppy	Not athletic enough
Too clumsy	Not pretty enough

Myth: "If I could be that very perfect child, I could make my parents' lives better."

By trying to be perfect, we cut off parts of ourselves.

4. Identify, as well as you can, what parts of yourself you cut off in order to please people. What parts of yourself did you have trouble accepting as a result of negative messages? Make notes.

_____

_____

_____

_____

_____

_____

_____

_____

_____

ACTIVITY 2.10
POLARITIES

Note To The Leader

Lost parts of oneself can include both positive and negative traits. In the book, *Enhancing Self Esteem* on page 110, the idea of polarities or dualities present within each of us is introduced. This activity will help identify both unowned areas of strength and weakness. Remember that even for so-called negative qualities there is always a context within which this trait could be useful. Every aspect of oneself is a potential resource. The following activity provides some practice in identifying lost aspects of oneself and finding ways that such qualities might be of benefit to self.

Background Information

We can get in touch with lost parts of ourselves by examining the polar opposites of how we see ourselves. In this way, we can enlarge our self-view.

Purposes

1. To examine polar opposites of ourself.

2. To enlarge our self-view.

Time Required

30 minutes

Participants

Any number; adolescents and adults

Materials Needed

Paper and pen

Procedure

1. Write six adjectives to describe how you see yourself. Next to each write what in your opinion would be the opposite of each.

Adjectives	Opposites
Example: Sensitive	Callous
_____	_____
_____	_____
_____	_____
_____	_____

2. Identify your objection to each of these opposites.

Opposites	Objections
a. _____	_____
b. _____	_____
c. _____	_____
d. _____	_____
e. _____	_____
f. _____	_____

Each of your objections represents a block to your developing this side of the polarity.

3. Try to identify the rule or rules associated with each opposite.

Opposites	Rules
a. _____	_____
b. _____	_____
c. _____	_____
d. _____	_____
e. _____	_____
f. _____	_____

4. For each of your opposite characteristics, come up with one instance when this quality might be useful to you.

a. _____	_____
b. _____	_____
c. _____	_____
d. _____	_____
e. _____	_____
f. _____	_____

ACTIVITY 2.11
REFUTING THE INNER CRITIC

Purposes

1. To maintain positive self-esteem by being watchful of the negative self-critic which often serves to reduce strides made in improving self-esteem.

2. To learn four guidelines are helpful in disarming this inner critic.

Time Required

5 to 10 minutes, several times a day

Participants

Intermediate grade school children, adolescents, or adults on individual or group settings

Materials Needed

None

Procedure

1. Utilize the following four guidelines to refute your inner critic:

    a. Rebuttal statements in one's mind must be forceful. The inner critic is strong and experienced. It has had many years of delivering negative messages to you. Your refutation needs to be equal or greater in force than the self-critic. Use the Howitzer Mantras, as described in an earlier technique, or develop a strong statement yourself. Your statement could be a strong "NO!".

    b. Rebuttal statements should be nonjudgmental. Avoid using pejorative adjectives and adverbs such as "awful, horrible, revolting." Avoid the concept of right or wrong. Instead concentrate on what is. One is not "stupid." It could be you got a C on a test, but this does not make you stupid.

    c. Be specific in refuting the self-critic. Avoid saying, "No one likes me." A specific statement might be, "Of the last five people I invited to a social event with me, two would not go." Focus on the facts.

    d. Balance the rebuttal to avoid selective perception. For example, instead of saying "Six people didn't come to my party," one could say "Six people did not come to my party, but four people did and they said they enjoyed themselves". Balance the negative and the positive. Often people with low self-esteem tend to perceive only the negative.

2. Apply these guidelines to your inner critic consistently for one week.

3. Review the results at the end of the week.

4. Process the learning and write your comments in the space provided.

5. Continue to use these guidelines for thirty consecutive days.

ACTIVITY 2.12
STROKE ECONOMY

Note To The Leader

Review in the book, *Enhancing Self Esteem*, pages 92-94 where the rules of the stroke economy are discussed. Reflect on your thoughts about each rule and evaluate whether each of these rules is operative in your family, work, or other environments. Many of us live in rather critical environments and are stroke deprived. Stroke deprived individuals also tend to malnourish others around them. In this next activity participants are invited to challenge some of these rules. Each of us has the power to create more nourishing environments.

Background Information

By violating the rules of the stroke economy we can more readily be in touch with our strengths and help others to be more aware of theirs.

Purpose

To challenge rules of the stroke economy.

Time Required

45 minutes

Participants

Any number: adolescents and/or adults

Materials Needed

Paper and pen

Procedure

1. Review the five rules of the stroke economy.

   > DON'T STROKE OTHERS.
   > DON'T ACCEPT STROKES.
   > DON'T REJECT STROKES.
   > DON'T ASK FOR STROKES.
   > DON'T STROKE YOURSELF.

2. Write how freely you are able to express appreciation, affection, and encouragement to others.

   _____

   _____

   _____

   _____

3. Write how fully you absorb strokes others give to you (physical, emotional, intellectual, social, spiritual).

_____

_____

_____

_____

_____

4. Think about strokes you have received and identify those which are easier to accept than others.

_____

_____

_____

_____

_____

5. Summarize how you are able to reject strokes, if you are, which you do not want.

_____

_____

_____

_____

_____

6. Summarize how willing you are to ask for the strokes that you want or if not, why not. (We can significantly increase our chances of getting what we want if we learn to ask.)

_____

_____

_____

_____

_____

7. Summarize how freely you are able to speak positively about yourself.

_____

_____

_____

_____

_____

8. Identify rules that block your ability to speak positively about yourself.

_____

_____

_____

_____

_____

9. Discuss the rules of the stroke economy with your group or with family and friends. How have you limited yourselves? What merit can you find in breaking these rules?

_____

_____

_____

_____

_____

10. Choose one rule of the stroke economy to practice breaking this week. Record instances when you violate the rule, describe the reactions of others and record your own feelings and thoughts as well. Report your findings to your group or friends.

_____

_____

_____

_____

_____

Variation in Procedure

This activity also could be done within a family, group, or classroom allowing time for people to experiment with breaking different rules and then processing reactions.

ACTIVITY 2.13
PROJECTION EXERCISE

Note To The Leader

In Chapter 4 of the book, *Enhancing Self Esteem*, the major defense mechanisms are reviewed. Read pages 123-127 and pay particular attention to the information on projection.

Background Information

Interpersonal conflict frequently involves a mutual projection process. By sorting out and owing projections, one can resolve many conflicts and increase self-awareness. By working through problems in relationships one can learn a lot about self.

Many interpersonal difficulties result from our inability to accept parts of ourselves. We then project these disowned qualities onto others and react negatively to them.

Purpose

To begin to reown some of our projections.

Time Required

15 minutes

Participants

Any number; adolescents and/or adults

Materials Needed

Paper and pen

Procedure

1. Think of someone towards whom you feel critical.

   _____

   _____

   _____

2. Identify those traits or behaviors/attitudes in this person that are the object of your criticism. Examples: controlling, sloppy.

   _____

   _____

   _____

3. Write what you would consider as the opposite of these traits/behaviors/attitudes? Example: free, tidy, well kept.

_____

_____

_____

4. Identify which traits, behaviors/attitudes, or their opposites listed in Items 2 and 3 are you also critical of yourself.

_____

_____

_____

5. Review response to Item 4 and see if you can own any of these traits/behaviors/attitudes you criticize in others. Have you ever in your life exhibited these?

_____

_____

_____

ACTIVITY 2.14
STRENGTH EXCHANGE

Note To The Leader

Review pages 188-192 in *Enhancing Self-Esteem* before doing this activity.

Purposes

1. To assist individuals to gain experience in giving and receiving positive feedback.

2. To learn how perceptions of self match the perceptions of others.

Time Required

Approximately 45 minutes, depending on the size of the group (This activity can be done in an individual setting and takes approximately ten minutes.)

Participants

Children (intermediate grades and above) and/or adults

Materials Needed

Paper and pencil for each participant and a small box or folder

Procedure

1. Sit in a circle with one person at a time volunteering to sit in the middle of the circle.

2. Write three strengths you believe the person sitting in the middle has. (Allow no talking during this time.)

3. When all participants have finished their responses, put them in the box or folder which is beside the volunteer in the middle of the circle.

4. Ask each volunteer to refrain from reading his or her feedback until everyone had a chance to sit in the middle of the circle.

5. Repeat the procedure until everyone has volunteered to be in the middle of the circle.

6. After everyone has received feedback about their personal strengths, write three strengths you believe you have.

7. Open your box or folder with the feedback in it.

8. Ask others questions about the feedback you received if you wish to do so.

9. Write how your ideas about strengths you have (responses to Item 6) compared to those received from others.

ACTIVITY 2.15
SELF-ESTEEM LEARNING EXCHANGE

Purposes

1. To help individuals learn how to experience various self-estimates through learning from others.

2. To practice and improve asking for what is needed in the area of self improvement in self-esteem.

Participants

Children (age eight or older) and/or adults in a group setting

Materials Needed

Pencil and a 3" by 5" index card for each person

Procedure

1. Write on the 3" by 5" card your name and one or two aspects of yourself which you consider to be positive (positive self-estimates, as described in Chapter 1). It could be, for example, that one person considers self to have good athletic skill. Another person might believe that he or she is good at making friends.

2. Have one-half of the participants to agree to try to teach their positive aspects to others and have them place their cards in the middle of the room.

3. Have the other one-half of the participants go to the cards and each select one positive aspect they would like to learn.

4. Have the person who selected the card join the person who wrote the card and they write together for a while as one teaches the other person the way he or she developed the positive aspect of self.

5. When finished, repeat Items 2, 3, and 4 with the other one-half of the participants placing their cards in the middle of the room.

6. After each person has a chance to learn how to develop a particular positive self aspect and a chance to teach the development of positive self aspect, have the large group then convene and discuss what they learned from each other.

7. Write what you learned.

_____

_____

_____

_____

PART III

NURTURANCE PHASE

Helping Professional

In the nurturance phase, the techniques assist individuals to nurture their newly found identity with its strengths and weakness patterns. The first two phases within themselves are not sufficient, as newly found self-esteem can be lost if it is not nurtured. Helping individuals to nurture themselves assists them to enhance strengths and minimize weaknesses.

Participant

In this section of your workbook you will learn how to continue developing your self-esteem. You will learn how to manage your self-talk, how to develop more friends, how to deal with criticism, and many other things. All these learnings are important in helping you to continue to improve your self-esteem.

ACTIVITY 3.1
LEGACY

Note To The Leader

Pages 63-70 in the book, *Enhancing Self Esteem*, introduces you to ideas about how experiences in one's family of origin may influence how a person feels about self today. Review this material before completing the following activity.

Purpose

To help you get in touch with patterns of self-attitudes and self-care you developed outside of your awareness through identification with early caregivers.

Time Required

30 to 45 minutes

Participants

Any number; adolescents and/or adults

Materials Needed

Paper and pen

Procedure

1. Write your responses to the following questions.

    a. Think for a minute about your primary same sex caretaker or person with whom you heavily identified. What kinds of things does/did (s)he say about him/herself

    —about his/her body? _____

    _____

    _____

    —about his/her ability to feel close? _____

    _____

    _____

    —about his/her intelligence? _____

    _____

    _____

    —about his/her ability to make decisions? _____

    _____

    _____

b. How does (s)he take care of or feed his/her body—good food, exercise, baths, oils, nice clothes, jewelry, hair?

_____

_____

_____

c. How does (s)he take care of or feed his or her mind—school, books, plays, travel, etc.?

_____

_____

_____

d. How does (s)he take care of or feed his or her emotional life—close, supportive, loving, friends, family?

_____

_____

_____

e. What feelings does (s)he express directly? Anger? Fear? Joy? Sadness?

_____

_____

_____

f. Does (s)he own and appreciate his/her sexuality?

_____

_____

_____

g. Is (s)he spiritual and does (s)he find comfort in this?

_____

_____

_____

h. How are you like this?

_____

_____

_____

2. Discuss your answers to Item 1 with a partner and have the partner share his or her answers with you.

3. Think of 3 scenes—3 common internal pictures you have of your same sex caregiver.

   For Example:

   —in kitchen making us coffee
   —cleaning, doing chores, engaged in hobbies
   —laughing and being playful
   —arguing with a family member

   Are these scenes familiar in <u>your</u> life as well? Are you behaving like your same sex caregiver?

   _____

   _____

   _____

   _____

   _____

4. Describe your same sex caregiver's personality. Chose 5-6 adjectives.

   _____

   _____

   _____

   _____

   _____

5. Identify which of the characteristics in Item 4 you see in yourself.

   _____

   _____

   _____

   _____

6. Choose words to describe how other people treat your same sex caregiver, e.g., respectful, distant, put him/her down?

   _____

   _____

   _____

   _____

   _____

7.   Record your same sex caregiver's position in his or her family.

    For example:

            first born girl child with 7 other kids
            last born boy of 3 children
            last born girl with 3 older boys
            middle boy with an older and a younger brother

    _____

    _____

8.   Think about how your same sex caregiver's family position affected him
     or her. What is your family position? How did it affect you?

    _____

    _____

    _____

    _____

    _____

ACTIVITY 3.2
BODY MAP

Note To The Leader

In Chapter 9, pp. 323-327, in the book, *Enhancing Self Esteem*, the importance of reconnecting with one's body is discussed.

Background Information

Many people have grown quite detached from their bodies and have, thereby, lost an important source of information which is crucial to identifying and meeting feelings and needs. This activity helps support a reconnection with your body. It is particularly helpful for those with eating disorders or other addictions as well as others who have low awareness of body sensation. For best results, the activity should initially be repeated daily at different points during the day and later at spaced intervals. When done repeatedly, it can be completed alone and small figures drawn in a body log.

Purposes

1. To enable you to increase body awareness.

2. To help you to connect better with your feelings as well as take better care of your bodily needs.

Time Required

45 minutes

Participants

Adolescents and/or adults

Materials Needed

One or preferably two sheets of paper approximately 30" by 78" for each participant, plus colored markers and crayons.

Procedure

1. Tear off a sheet of paper the length of your body. Find a partner. One partner lies on paper while the other partner traces body. Be sure to trace front on one side of paper and back on the other side or a second sheet of paper if you have two sheets.

2. Silently and alone, take your two body outlines to a private spot. Use crayons/pastels to chart your body energy . . . use a different color for each of the following:

> energy streamings and vibrations
> tension spots
> pain

hot spots
tingling, prickling
cold spots
numb areas

3. Go through your entire body expressing feelings associated with various body parts. On your drawing, write these feelings next to each body part in which you experience sensation.

4. Discuss your drawing with your partner and then answer the questions.

    a.   What did you discover about yourself?

_____

_____

_____

    b.   Were you more aware of sensations in the front of your body or the back?

_____

    c.   Which areas did you skip over?

_____

_____

    d.   In which body areas did you experience most sensation?

_____

    e.   Least sensation?

_____

    f.   What messages and memories do you associate with each area?

_____

_____

_____

_____

    g.   How did you feel throughout the activity?

_____

_____

ACTIVITY 3.3
REACH OUT AND TOUCH SOMEONE

Note To The Leader

A support system is a very important element in nurturing self-esteem, (Read pages 69-73 and 200-201 in *Enhancing Self-Esteem*). This activity helps one to understand different ways of reaching out to others.

Background Information

Everyone needs to reach out to others. People frequently hold themselves back from support of others because they don't want to appear ridiculous or intrusive. Often people have strong needs to reach out to others but they do not because they feel awkward, embarrassed, uncertain, or unworthy. Making contact with others, however, is a learned skill, with practice this becomes easier and the result is a more extensive support system.

Purposes

1. To highlight the importance of interpersonal relationships in enhancing self-esteem.

2. To provide an opportunity to experiment with different methods of reaching out to others.

Time Required

20 to 30 minutes

Participants

Middle school and high school students, and adults in a classroom or individual setting

Materials Needed

Paper and pencil

Procedure

1. Ask everyone to stand up and move around the room.

2. During a five minute interval ask people to make contact with five other people, this can be done in whatever way they wish.

3. After five minutes ask the group to reassemble.

4. Ask each person to complete these questions for himself or herself.

    a.   What did you notice about your contacts?

    _____

    _____

b.	Did you initiate contact or were you hoping others would contact you?

_____

_____

c.	Who talked, who listened?

_____

_____

d.	What was your eye contact like?

_____

_____

e.	Was your style similar or different from your usual style of reaching out to others?

_____

_____

5.	Share some of your ideas with the group. (If you are doing this individually, you may be doing it between counseling sessions. If so, share the result with your counselor, teacher, or school psychologist.)

6.	Perform round two of this activity where each person is asked to again reach out to five people during a five minute time interval. In the first round, most likely people were cautious and hesitant about how they did this.

7.	This time ask people to assume they are a person of high self-esteem. They are asked to break their normal rules for reaching out.

8.	After completing the activity, complete these questions:

a.	What was the energy level like compared to the first time?

_____

_____

b.	In which approach did you feel most free?

_____

_____

c.	What was most inhibiting?

_____

_____

d.   What prevents you from interacting in this way in everyday life?

_____

_____   _____

e.   How could you change your behavior in interacting with others?

_____

_____

ACTIVITY 3.4
FEELING SENSATIONS

Note To The Leader

Read pages 328-335, in the book *Enhancing Self Esteem*, before proceeding with this activity.

Background Information

Every one of our feeling states is grounded in a body experience of particular sensations. For various individuals, idiosyncratic differences may be in those sensations. One person, when angry, may experience more tension in the jaw, another's anger may be focused in constriction of muscles around the eyes, for example. By becoming aware of how you express your emotions through specific sensations, these sensations can then become cues for you in reconnecting with your feelings.

Purposes

1. To enable you to identify your feelings more easily thereby enabling you to meet your needs.

2. To help you identify the physical accompaniments of your feelings so that you can begin to use these physical sensations and signals to more accurately identify your feelings.

Time Required

30 minutes

Participants

Adolescents and/or adults

Material Needed

Pen

Procedure

1. Notice the physical components (examples: tightening, tension, temperature changes, softening, changes in breathing—rapid, shallow, deep—heart rate, perspiration) of your feelings as you reflect on the following:

    a. SADNESS

    Think of someone who has been very important to you but who is no longer in your life now (through death, separation, divorce). See that person standing before you. Remember that person's face. Call back some memories of special times you had together. Replay these. Now see this person slowly turn and walk away. What are you aware of in your body? Notice your breathing, your eyes, your chest. Record your physical reactions.

_____

_____

_____

_____

_____

b. ANGER

Remember a time someone violated you, accused you unjustly, cheated you out of something, treated you unfairly in some way. Who comes to mind? What happened? As you think of this, what are you aware of in your body? Notice your jaw, muscles around your eyes, hands, mouth, nostrils. Record your physical sensations.

_____

_____

_____

_____

_____

c. EXCITEMENT

Imagine a time when you took a big risk, tried something daring—broke a rule—tried something new, gone somewhere you'd never been—in work, play, travel—any area whatsoever. What do you notice about your breathing? The rest of your body? Record your physical sensations.

_____

_____

_____

_____

_____

d. FEAR

Remember a time you felt highly threatened, in danger—physically or emotionally. Relive the experience as fully as you can. Where are you? Who are you with? What is happening? What do you notice in your body as you recapture this feeling. Record your physical sensations.

_____

_____

_____

_____

_____

2. Describe how sensitive you are to changes in your body.

_____

_____

_____

_____

_____

3. Identify those parts of your body of which you are most aware.

_____

_____

_____

_____

_____

4. Identify those parts of your body of which you are least aware.

_____

_____

_____

_____

_____

5. Describe those feelings that you are most able to experience.

_____

_____

_____

_____

_____

6. Describe those feelings that you are least able to experience.

_____

_____

_____

_____

_____

ACTIVITY 3.5
THE WORTHY YOU

Note To The Leader

Pages 133-134 and 141-144 of the book entitled *Enhancing Self Esteem* will help prepare you to make the tape needed in this activity. Following reading of the material, proceed to the activity.

Background Information

Many people unconsciously play negative, self-critical tapes in their heads. This is a habit pattern which needs to be broken and replaced with a new, more self-enhancing tape.

We all have the capacity to see ourselves as pure and precious beings at sometime in our lives. Here we ask you to focus on an age when you believe you were most pure and worthy of love.

Purpose

To help you expand on this good feeling you had when you were most pure and worthy of love.

Time Required

30 minutes

Participants

Any age

Materials Needed

Crayons, pastels, paints, or colored pencils

Procedure

1. Draw a picture of yourself at whatever age you consider yourself to have been most pure and worthy of love. Use crayons for this drawing. Place yourself in a safe, comfortable surrounding. Surround the entire area with a golden light of protection.

2. Send the child messages of his/her inherent goodness, spontaneity, and creativity.

3. Now write these messages on your drawing.

4. Record your feelings once you have completed the activity. Refer to your picture any time you feel bad about yourself or need a reminder of your basic worth and lovableness.

_____

_____

_____

_____

_____

_____

_____

_____

_____

_____

ACTIVITY 3.6
EVALUATING A FRIENDSHIP SYSTEM

Note To The Leader

Review pages 69-73, in the book *Enhancing Self Esteem*, regarding the discussion on support networks. This will give you background for assisting others through this activity.

Background Information

Individuals with high self esteem are in touch with both their inner resources and their interpersonal resources. This activity will help you to identify specific ways that you can strengthen your friendships.

Creating a nurturing friendship system is an essential ingredient of a happy life.

Purpose

To assess the quality of your friendship network.

Time Required

20 minutes

Participants

Adolescents and/or adults

Material Needed

Pen

Procedure

1. List 5 qualities you value in a friend. Rank order these.

   a. _____

   b. _____

   c. _____

   d. _____

   e. _____

2. List the friends in your inner circle. Which qualities and behaviors in Item 1 do they possess?

	Friends	Qualities & Behaviors Possessed
a.	_____	_____
b.	_____	_____
c.	_____	_____
d.	_____	_____
e.	_____	_____

3. Identify your closest friends.

a. _____

b. _____

c. _____

4. Recall and record phases that those relationships went through.

_____

_____

_____

_____

_____

5. Think of and write how you can bring someone in your outer circle of friends closer.

_____

_____

_____

_____

_____

ACTIVITY 3.7
TREASURE CHEST

Note To The Leader

Review pages 92-94, in the book *Enhancing Self Esteem*, regarding rules of the stroke economy before completing this activity.

Background Information

Many people are averse to stroking or complimenting themselves. They call this bragging or "having a big head". Oftentimes people are put-down if they speak well of themselves giving the idea that something is wrong with appreciating themselves. If you don't think highly of yourself, who will? As long as it is not overdone, bragging is very healthy. Knowing what you do well helps others to identify you as a resource in particular areas and can build others' confidence in you.

Purposes

1. To reinforce positive self-attributes.

2. To teach a method for healing the inner needy self.

3. To foster internal nourishment.

Time Required

15 minutes

Participants

Adolescents and or adults

Material Needed

Pen

Procedure

1. Allow your eyes to gently close and be in touch with your breathing. Be aware of your breath slowly moving in and out—through your nostrils, your mouth—breathing deeply, fully, filling your body with warm, nurturing air.

2. Take a few moments to appreciate your body for the fine work that it does . . . Your heart beats, your organs function, your body moves with coordination—all without your trying.

3. Breathe in deeply now as you reflect on all that you appreciate. Now exhale completely, expelling the last bit of air slowly out your mouth and nose.

4. Pay attention to a place about 2 inches below your navel—the center of your being—imagine breathing in and out through this spot. With each breath feeling more and more secure, more and more relaxed.

5. Now slowly travel to that place deep inside where you keep that special treasure that is called by your name. Your treasure chest of self worth is filled with many riches—some of them known to you; some hidden.

6. Picture the treasure chest. How big is it? What is it made of?

7. Allow yourself the opportunity to look inside. Does the lid open easily? What special gifts does it hold?

8. Carefully look through all the treasures in your chest. Notice how you feel as you examine each of your finds. Describe each of them. Each gift is a symbol of something you might appreciate in yourself.

9. Make a mental picture of yourself and tell that image what you are now in touch with, thus, appreciating about yourself. Notice how easy or difficult this is for you. Deliver your messages slowly. Look into your eyes as you do this. Notice the facial expression of your mirror-image self. Be aware of your breathing as you take in these messages.

10. List each of the findings in your treasure chest and describe each with four adjectives.

   a. _____
   _____
   _____

   b. _____
   _____
   _____

   c. _____
   _____
   _____

   d. _____
   _____
   _____

   e. _____
   _____
   _____

11. Identify personal qualities each finding represents.

a. _____

b. _____

c. _____

d. _____

e. _____

12. Describe how you feel about your findings. Can you accept the personal qualities identified in Item 11?

_____

_____

_____

_____

_____

ACTIVITY 3.8
ESTEEM BUILDING INVENTORY

Background Information

With the many demands that ordinary life places upon us, an important procedure is for each of us to build into our daily lives a variety of self-care activities as well as other experiences which bring us joy. While some people reserve portions of weekends for their hobbies and interests, for maximum benefit we suggest that you sprinkle your weekdays with fun activities as well. Even 30 minutes a day can make a big differences in how you feel.

Through this written activity, participants survey a variety of sources for self-gratification.

Purposes

1. To emphasize the importance of a wide spectrum of positive resources in oneself, in others, and in activities.

2. To help spot areas of deficiency which may need to be strengthened.

Time Required

30 minutes

Participants

Adolescents and/or adults

Material Needed

Pen

Procedure

1. List six aspects of your personality that you really like and are proud to let others see (examples: direct, loyal, creative, spontaneous, bright).

    a. _____

    b. _____

    c. _____

    d. _____

    e. _____

    f. _____

2. List ten of your favorite things to do (examples: gardening, reading, listening to music).

   a. _____

   b. _____

   c. _____

   d. _____

   e. _____

   f. _____

   g. _____

   h. _____

   i. _____

   j. _____

3. List five ways you support yourself emotionally (examples: weekly Men's/Women's group, regular dinners or lunches with friends with whom I can open up, personal growth group, regular vacations away, journal keeping).

   a. _____

   b. _____

   c. _____

   d. _____

   e. _____

4. List five ways you attend to your body (examples: racquetball and/or weight-training five times per week, hot tubbing, massages, regular physicals, relaxation exercises).

   a. _____

   b. _____

   c. _____

   d. _____

   e. _____

5. List four ways you attend to your spiritual life (examples: daily meditation, spiritual reading, spiritual discussions with friends).

a. _____

b. _____

c. _____

d. _____

6. List the people from each period of your life who taught you most about self care and describe what each taught you (examples; Kerry—taught me to enjoy sports, Virginia—helped me to be gentler with myself and more forgiving).

a. Childhood _____

_____

_____

b. Adolescence _____

_____

_____

c. Young adulthood _____

_____

_____

d. Middle years _____

_____

_____

e. Later years _____

_____

_____

7. List the places where you have felt most relaxed, nurtured.

_____

_____

_____

8. Describe your most powerful spiritual experience.

   _____

   _____

   _____

9. List four ways you stimulate your intellect or creativity (examples: workshops, reading, joint work projects with friends).

   a. _____

   b. _____

   c. _____

   d. _____

10. Identify, by reviewing your answers, which areas you need to strengthen in order to more fully nurture yourself?

    a. _____

    b. _____

    c. _____

    d. _____

11. For each of two responses to Item 10, set one specific goal to further strengthen that area within the next month.

    a. _____

       _____

       _____

    b. _____

       _____

       _____

ACTIVITY 3.9
FAMILY CLIMATE

Note To The Leader

Review the family norms/family rules, pages 68-70, in the book *Enhancing Self Esteem*, before doing this activity on family climate.

Background Information

Many people say that their home is their refuge. Yet, your refuge may become yet another source of stress. Rather than continuing to perpetuate destructive or non-productive patterns, take the time to evaluate your family and work on changes to help strengthen your family. Your family can be a powerful and positive source of support.

Purposes

1. To help you characterize and evaluate the climate of your family.

2. To help you determine how nurturing your family can be meaningful to you.

3. To help you decide how much time to spend with your family or what changes you might like to instigate in order for your family to be more nurturing to you.

Time Required

30 minutes

Participants

Adolescents and/or adults

Materials Needed

Paper and pen

Procedure

1. Describe what or how you enjoy being with your family.

   _____

   _____

   _____

   _____

   _____

   _____

   _____

2. Think about how your family members like and trust each other.

_____

_____

_____

_____

_____

_____

_____

3. Describe what makes your family members trustworthy.

_____

_____

_____

_____

_____

_____

_____

4. Recall some of the most fun times in your family and summarize how you have fun together.

_____

_____

_____

_____

_____

_____

_____

5. Think about those times when you felt you were listened to the most and give a couple of examples.

_____

_____

_____

_____

_____

_____

_____

6. Recall those times when family members were very honest, dependable and good examples.

_____

_____

_____

_____

_____

_____

_____

_____

_____

_____

7. Think about those times in your family when touching was permitted and nurtured. Then describe effects on those involved.

_____

_____

_____

_____

_____

_____

_____

_____

_____

_____

8. Characterize what occurs within the family when a mistake occurs by one of the family members.

_____

_____

_____

_____

_____

_____

_____

_____

_____

9. Check between each pair of words to rate how you experience your family. What is it like to be in your family?

cold — — — — — — — — — — hot

rigid — — — — — — — — — — flexible

polite — — — — — — — — — — real

boring — — — — — — — — — — lively

chaotic — — — — — — — — — — organized

tense — — — — — — — — — — relaxed

distant — — — — — — — — — — close

secrecy — — — — — — — — — — openness

dry — — — — — — — — — — emotional

loud — — — — — — — — — — quiet

10. By using a metaphor describe how you experience your family and why. (For example, my family is like a car; I can't live without them, yet I can't live with them.)

_____

_____

_____

_____

_____

11. Summarize your feelings inside when you're with your family.

List physical symptoms	List emotional reactions
headaches	warm, close
queasy stomach	relaxed
aching neck and shoulders	comfortable
	excited
	happy
	angry
	fearful
	lonely

_____   _____

_____   _____

_____   _____

_____   _____

_____   _____

12. Identify as well as you can, what the physical symptoms and emotional reactions listed in Item 11 are.

_____

_____

_____

_____

_____

_____

13. In your mind's eye, paint a picture as you think about your family.

Do they look happy/sad?

Tight/slouchy?   Who looks how?

Are their faces blank, or full of expression?

14. Summarize in words your picture from Item 13.

_____

_____

_____

_____

_____

_____

15. Discuss your responses with one other person. How do your families compare?

_____

_____

_____

_____

_____

_____

16. Identify how you would like your family to be different.

_____

_____

_____

_____

_____

_____

17. Describe how you could help bring about that change.

_____

_____

_____

_____

_____

18. Make a contract with yourself and perhaps with the person you shared in Item 15 to talk to at least one family member about some of what you discovered.

_____

_____

_____

_____

_____

ACTIVITY 3.10
GRATEFULNESS

Note To The Leader

Review the description of the Cycle of Experience on pages 108-116 in the book *Enhancing Self Esteem*, paying particular attention to the last stages of the cycle—contact, affirmation, and withdrawal. These later phases often are not given full attention in Western culture. Read the section "Stilling the Mind" as well (pages 140-141). When you have completed this, continue with the next activity. This activity will help you attend to contact and affirmation, helping you to absorb your positive experiences more fully.

Background Information

By highlighting how we are blessed, we can make ourselves all the richer. One way to practice receiving is to pay attention to even the simplest, smallest thing we appreciate—a sunny day, the sound of birds chirping, a kind word from a customer, a smile from a stranger, all the little things for which you are grateful. All too infrequently do we stop and count our blessings. Yet, life has so much for which we can be thankful.

Purpose

To take time to note some positive things in life.

Time Required

45 minutes

Participants

Any number: all ages

Materials Needed

Pen, paper, crayons

Procedure

1. Use the space provided to note your blessings.

    For example:
    Morning—sunny day
        —good breakfast
        —waking up feeling great
        —the ability to coordinate the household chores and responsibilities with school work, and manage to get to work on time
        —my friend's greeting when I came in

a.   MORNING: _____

_____

_____

_____

b.   AFTERNOON: _____

_____

_____

_____

c.   EVENING: _____

_____

_____

_____

Note—Children in a classroom at the end of morning and afternoon sessions might be asked to make small drawings representing the little things which happened during that period for which they are grateful. Even adults might find drawings helpful in more deeply implanting the positive focus.

2.   Record how you feel at the end of this day.

_____

_____

_____

_____

_____

_____

_____

ACTIVITY 3.11
RESOURCE WHEEL

Background Information

Not only do people currently in your life help support your self-esteem but also those who have nurtured you in the past are useful in bolstering positive feelings about yourself. All those who provided support bring with them certain attitudes and skills which can help you cope with daily life. Many of these qualities you have integrated into your own behavioral repertoire so that even when these people are not in your current life, you carry them with you through what you learned from them. The more aware you are of your resources, the better your coping and the higher your self-esteem.

Purpose

To identify people (past and present) who can be resources that you can draw upon in times of need.

Time Required

20 minutes

Participants

Any age

Material Needed

Pen

Procedure

1. Imagine yourself surrounded by people in your life who have nurtured you physically, emotionally, or spiritually.

2. List each person in a circle and select one or two words to describe how each person behaved towards you—for example,

    Aunt Jenny: warm, fun-loving
    Mrs. Dreikurs: encouraging, sensitive

3. Review your resource wheel and identify the gaps.

4. Set three goals to complete in the next three months and list from your resource wheel those who may assist you with each goal.

    a. _____

        _____

    b. _____

        _____

    c. _____

        _____

Church

Others
(clubs, organizations, etc.)

_____ : _____   _____ : _____
_____ : _____   _____ : _____
_____ : _____   _____ : _____
_____ : _____   _____ : _____

Adult Friends of
Family or Parents
of Friends, Adult
Neightbors

Your Name

Teachers

_____ : _____   _____   _____ : _____
_____ : _____   _____ : _____
_____ : _____   _____ : _____
_____ : _____   _____ : _____

Friends

Family

_____ : _____   _____ : _____
_____ : _____   _____ : _____
_____ : _____   _____ : _____
_____ : _____   _____ : _____

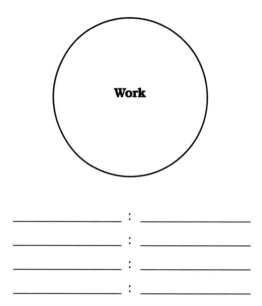

_____ : _____
_____ : _____
_____ : _____
_____ : _____

Activity 3.12
FANTASY:
NURTURING THE CHILD OF YOUR PAST

Note to the Leader

Review pages 137-139 in the book, *Enhancing Self* Esteem, and this entire activity before beginning it. Make sure you have the necessary materials and a quiet, comfortable environment where participants will not be disturbed. Many participants may want to lie down during the activity. (Remove contact lenses.)

Background Information

Problems with self-esteem often stem from incidents of rejection, abandonment, abuse or neglect in childhood. At those times, if you had no one to help you cope with such negative experiences your self-esteem may have been extremely battered. A succession of such incidents can produce a flawed sense of self which may require healing. If this activity is being done on your own outside of participation in a group, then, find a trusted person who is willing to read the following fantasy to you. Pick a quiet, comfortable environment where you won't be disturbed. You may wish to lie down.

Purpose

To help heal the wounded child within. This activity is useful for anyone who has suffered trauma in their lives—particularly childhood trauma.

Time Required

1 hour

Participants

Any number: adolescents and adults

Setting

Office or classroom

Materials Needed

1. Tape player
2. Halpern, Steven. (1981). *Eventide* (Cassette Recording).
3. Williamson, Chris. (1985). *Snow Angel,* "Lullabye" (Cassette Recording). Oakland, CA: Olivia Records, Inc.
4. Paillard Chamber Orchestra. (1977). *The Pachelbel Canon,* (Cassette Recording). New York, NY: RCA Corporation.

You will need to prepare an audio tape with the above selections of music to correspond with the transcript.

Procedure

1. Play the cassette recording entitled "Eventide."

2. Read the following to the participant(s):

Arrange yourself as comfortably as possible. Focus on your breathing—breath with your *belly*—let your breath carry in calming energy as it finds its most comfortable rhythm . . . With each exhalation, release the tension in your body . . . breathing in and breathing out . . . Allow yourself to pause a moment after each exhalation and watch the calm of your being expand. Feel your peacefulness expand—like water rippling from a stone that has been lightly tossed into a calm lake—circles of ripples, reverberating relaxation. Your breath moves in and out, washing away more and more tension, like ocean waves, your breath washes away all the tightness and stress.

Now I'd like you to think of a personal symbol that represents this body relaxation . . . the symbol can be a color, a sound, a picture, a sensation . . . anything you want . . . You can use this symbol whenever you want to relax. Whenever you bring this symbol into your awareness, your whole body will begin to relax. Tell your body this now. Your body will come to know and love this symbol. Your body will respond to this symbol more and more quickly. Imagine this symbol now and feel any lingering tensions begin to melt away . . .

Give your mind the space now to calm down—to feel serene. I'd like you to imagine being in a place you find very, very peaceful—a place which feels good—it can be wherever you want—at the ocean, in the mountains, under a tree somewhere, in a meadow . . . wherever you like. It can be a place you've been—or you can make up an imaginary place where you feel very calm and relaxed. Let yourself be fully there in your mind. Use all your senses to really feel yourself there. Feel the air against your skin. *See* what's around you—colors, shapes—listen to the sounds of this very special place . . .

Imagine your body is like a sponge, soaking in all the peaceful feelings around you—breathe in the calm air, bringing in the serenity . . . breathing in and out . . . becoming more and more a part of this place—feeling very good to be a part of it all. Your mind has quieted down—and yet is very alert. As you are in this state of inner calm and peacefulness, I'd like you to imagine that you are of inner calm and peacefulness, I'd like you to imagine that you are a leaf upon a tree and that it's on a warm sunny afternoon. Feel a gentle breeze come along and lift you up. Feel yourself floating through the air as long as you like—floating—sailing gently with the breeze. When you're ready, slowly flutter down, your inner awareness becomes more and more aware of your life.

As you move down deeper into yourself, when you land upon the ground, you are going to land in a very special place where the limitations of time have disappeared. This is the autumn of time itself. Here you can re-experience and remake the seasons of your life.

This place has different qualities. It's a very magical place. Look around—soon you'll see, imagine, discover, or create a shelf—a mantelpiece with a mirror towards the back of it. This is a very special mantelpiece. Your imagination can use this mirror to reflect your life. When you look into the mirror, you can see all that has come before in your life—all that leads up to where you stand at this juncture in your life . . .

If you choose, you can enter the looking glass and go back into your past. You can go back and view it with what you know now, learning more as you view it once again, with all your life experience. You'll find that you'll carry your past around with you differently . . . Your wisdom will become wider and wider.

See the mirror before you . . . choose now if you'll enter— Now I'd like you to play back any particular time, event, or chapter of your life from your childhood past—that you carry *strong*, disturbing feelings about—something that still *upsets* you. Choose one particular scene, and just watch it unfold before you in the mirror . . . a scenario of the past. Just take a moment and watch it unfold. Watch yourself in the scene. How old are you? Picture yourself fully. Hear your voice. Tune into words, gestures, facial expressions of everyone in the scene. Where are you? Who is there with you? Look around . . . at the landscape, sights, sounds, furniture, shape of the room—are there any familiar smells? Take in whatever is there—Watch it as if you were watching a movie of someone else's life. Watch everyone, watch it unfold as it did unfold . . . Replay it in the mirror on the mantle, the mantle of the past . . .

Now replay the scene once again . . . notice how you felt, what you believed about yourself . . . about others . . . what you believed was possible at the time. . . Notice which aspects of who you are were prominent . . . remember what you decided at the time. . . notice if you felt victimized . . . if you had given up your power . . . or if you weren't taking into account where any of the other participants in the scene were coming from. What were you needing back then? What skills or resources inside yourself? What help from others did you need?

3. Change Music Now to Pachelbel

I'd like you to imagine a most nurturing person approaching you at that time—the person may be someone you know or may be imaginary. See this person approaching you at a time when you so needed help— and care—and attention. Imagine yourself breaking through your "everything is fine" or "I don't need anyone" facade. Imagine reaching out and asking this nurturing person for help. This nurturing person's warm loving eyes help bridge your lack of trust and fear of disappointment. Take this in. You need only to utter a couple of words or even reach out with your eyes or hands or heart and this person is there for you . . . giving to you in exactly the way you're needing him/her right now . . . in any special way you want . . . with words and hugs, advice and reassurances . . . everything you've longed for . . . making sure you know that you're lovable *without even* trying. Hear the messages you need to hear . . . soak in the good feelings . . . Knowing that someone is very glad that you are in this world . . . Your nurturing friend is very happy to give to you and meet your needs . . . in any way you desire . . . likes to hold you *when you want or need that* . . . loves *to be there for you* and *follow your pace . . . meets your needs.* Take a few minutes to receive this care fully now . . . reach the deepest parts of you.

Long Pause

The words, *"You are OK as you are"* bring tears to your eyes. You find yourself breathing a deep sigh of relief as you realize *there is nothing you have to do to win this person's love* . . . allow yourself to bask in this warm, pure light of love . . . let it sink in . . . warming you right down to your bones . . . Knowing that you are *wanted, loved, protected,* and *supported* thoroughly . . .

4. Begin to play the cassette recording entitled "Lullabye." Play the entire song. This selection has words. Do not read further until this selection is completed.

5. After "Lullabye," begin to play the cassette recording entitled "Eventide."

You have all the resources you need now to begin transforming your childhood past. I'd like you to travel back to your past now once again. As you look into the mirror on the mantle, feel the soft light, reassuring support of your nurturing friend's hand upon your shoulder. As you replay the scene this time, accompanied by your nurturing, loving friend, see yourself letting go of the pain, the hurt, letting the disappointment drain out. Hear yourself expressing your feelings to those around you . . . Say everything you need to say . . . say it straight with all your feelings accompanying your message. If there are no words, that's OK too . . . just let all the feelings drain out in any way that fits . . . Feel the strength of your nurturing friend supporting you in releasing all that is there.

Imagine the emotional storm beginning to dissipate leaving behind clear, fresh cleansed air.

However you imagine this . . . send compassion back into that scene, compassion for yourself, for others . . . Know that you can heal your past, you can heal your memories. In fact as you give compassion to this episode of your life you *are* healing your past, and you are enriching who you are in the present. Know that this is so.

Acknowledge what you have learned from this chapter of your life. Experience the positive side of this episode. Imagine it as if it were a gift, a gift to your pool of wisdom . . . Allow yourself for a moment to appreciate this time in your life . . . what lesson has it given you? (Pause). Give yourself permission to accept the lesson. Let it settle into who you are.

Continue to focus on what you learned from this time, how you can grow from it. Let this time deepen your pool of wisdom . . . Bring the lesson into yourself, into your whole self, almost as though it were to become cellular knowledge . . . let it nourish who you are, gaining strength to move into the future. Bring lessons learned into the present so you can move into the future with greater poise . .

    and in so doing know that you can now let go, for you've gained the gift of the past.

You may want to imagine your past as a golden thread of your life. Let your past weave a golden robe of wisdom . . . Immerse yourself in wisdom . . . transform the weight, the baggage of the past into this golden robe and imagine being draped in it . . . As you let go of the past, embraced by the lessons it offers, you move into the future with grace, with ease, with foresight . . . a little lighter.

As you do this, become aware of what needs to be done in your daily activities in order to carry this energy, this movement into your life . . . embracing the lessons, letting go of the bad times, creating new spaces in your life. Let go of the past, creating space in the present to move into the future in new and liberating ways.

And imagine yourself doing whatever you need to do to have this occur in your present daily life. Feel yourself living with this newfound wisdom . . . Notice how it may affect those around you.

To return to your waking consciousness, all you need to do is to tell yourself, "I am now going to count from one to five." I will snap my fingers . . . at the count of five, you will open your eyes feeling revitalized and remembering all that you have experienced in this meditation . . . Count slowly, giving your consciousness time to adjust to levels, just as I am about to do . . .

> ONE—becoming more aware of the room around you . . .

> TWO—coming up slowly now . . .

> THREE—at the count of five you'll open your eyes feeling relaxed and refreshed, remembering all you've experienced . . .

> FOUR—coming up now . . . bringing with you your sense of well being . . .

> FIVE!—eyes open, feeling refreshed, revitalized, and relaxed, remembering all you have experienced . . . having brought with you your sense of well being.

(Leader snaps fingers)

Allow yourself to come out to outer levels of consciousness, know you can return to this inner world whenever you wish . . . Feel your eyelids flutter open—feel yourself revitalized, remembering all you've experienced and feeling a sense of well being that will carry over into your activities . . .

Note: Participants are generally deeply touched by this imagery experience. Encourage participants to make contact with those around them giving support in any way which fits. A break is often useful at this point before processing in dyads or triads, or doing journal work since it often takes people a while to come out of this deep state and be able to verbalize. Some will wish to keep the experience private in which case journaling might be an appropriate alternative.

From a "Healing Family Wounds" workshop, Peoplemaking Midwest, 1105 Watervliet Avenue, Dayton, Ohio 45420.

Resources for Activity 3.12

Halpern, Steven. (1981). "Eventide" (Cassette Recording). Belmont, CA: Halpern Sounds.

Paillard Chamber Orchestra. (1977). "Pachelbel: Canon" (Cassette Recording). New York, NY.

Peoplemaking Midwest. (February, 1987). "Healing Family Wounds" workshop. Peoplemaking Midwest, 1105 Watervliet Avenue, Dayton, OH 45420.

Williamson, Chris. (1985). Snow Angel, "Lullabye" (Cassette Recording). Oakland, CA: Olivia Records, Inc.

PART IV

MAINTENANCE PHASE

Helping Professional

In maintenance phase the following techniques are used to help maintain adequate self-esteem over time. Since self-esteem is a process of evolution, various aspects within the self change as one matures. Individuals need to learn how to maintain adequate self-esteem just as it is necessary to maintain a car, a house, or an interpersonal relationship if it is to grow or flourish. Techniques provided in the maintenance phase are interventions that help individuals to turn life experiences into learning situations, to set appropriate goals, to facilitate risk-taking, to forecast desired personal outcomes and to publicly affirm goals.

Participants

Finally in this part of the workbook you will learn how to keep high self-esteem as you grow older. Being able to effectively set goals, take risk, and do affirmations are some of the techniques which help you to do this.

ACTIVITY 4.1
SELF-MANDALA ASSESSMENT

(To be done only under the direction of a leader.)

Note To The Leader

Please review pages 215-218 in *Enhancing Self Esteem*. Also review Chapter 1 of that text.

Background Information

Numerous aspects of our lives require our attention if we are to improve and maintain self-esteem.

Purpose

To assess aspects of our lives and develop specific goals to assist in the maintenance process.

Time Required

30 minutes

Participants

Any number: adolescents and/or adults

Materials Needed

Paper and pen

Procedure

1. List the layers of the Self-Mandala, on pages 215-218 in *Enhancing Self Esteem* or from the items listed under number 4 of this activity, which are least developed in a positive way for you.

   _____

   _____

   _____

2. Think of something specific you can do next week to further develop each of the layers listed in Procedure No. 1.

   Examples: **Interactional**—At the next Investors Club meeting I will talk with at least two people I have never met before.

   Nutrition—I will eat at least two pieces of fruit each day.

   _____

   _____

   _____

3. Describe the impact of Procedure 2 on your self-esteem.

_____

_____

_____

4. On a monthly basis assess yourself using the Self-Mandala and develop goals for yourself in areas where you are slipping.

physical—body focus, sexuality, health

intellectual—stimulation and expansion of your cognitive abilities

emotional—all feeling states

sensual—awareness of all senses: olfactory, visual, kinesthetic, auditory, touch, taste

interactional—relationship style and communication skills and abilities

nutritional—includes anything ingested

contextual—environmental factors

spiritual—relationship with a higher power/higher self

ACTIVITY 4.2
SYMBOLS

Background Information

Symbols can be powerful anchors for states we wish to experience more in our lives. Such simple forms and images can quickly evoke states we want to remember and guide ourselves back to.

Purpose

To create symbols for several desired states.

Time Required

60 minutes

Participants

Any number: Adolescents and/or adults

Materials Needed

Paper and pen

Procedure

1. Create and draw a symbol for each of the following. Use color, form, texture to convey your experiences of each.

    a.   Balance

    b.   Stability

c.   Serenity

d.   Security

e.   Joy

f.   Other (Specify)

2. Pick one symbol to focus on each week. Make several copies of the symbol and place in visible areas in your environment (example, bedroom mirror, car, desk at work, refrigerator). Meditate on this symbol a few minutes each day. Note the feelings/sensations/images generated by this symbol as you do this.

_____

_____

_____

_____

_____

_____

_____

_____

_____

_____

ACTIVITY 4.3
DAILY FORGIVENESS

Background Information

Admitting when you are wrong is good guidance for healthy living. In this activity we ask you to take a daily inventory of any wrongs, make amends to others, and forgive yourself. In this way you can avoid carrying the guilt of our human errors.

Purposes

1. To take a daily inventory of any wrongs.

2. To make amends to others.

3. To forgive self for any wrongs or errors.

Time Required

30 minutes

Participants

Any number: older adolescents and adults

Materials Needed

Paper and pen

Procedure

1. Recall your activities for today and, as you do, ask yourself, "Is there any way you harmed someone today through thoughtlessness, blame, excessive criticism, or some other character flaw?" Give an example.

   _____

   _____

   _____

   _____

2. Answer the following questions.

   a. Did you admit to the person you harmed that you were wrong? Yes _____ No _____

   b. If not, will you? Yes _____ No _____

   c. If not, why not?

      _____

      _____

d. If you are planning to or already have admitted you were wrong, what will (did) you say?

_____

_____

_____

e. How did you feel as you did this or how do you expect you will feel when you do this?

_____

_____

_____

3. Summarize how well or to what extent you can accept your shortcomings and forgive yourself for your imperfections.

_____

_____

_____

_____

_____

4. Imagine yourself in a healing light. When you shower in the evening or in the morning, be in touch with the healing power of water to wash away any blame or guilt that you are carrying. Imagine each drop of water washing the pain away, releasing, forgiving, letting go.

5. After your shower, use some oil to conduct a simple blessing ritual. Begin to anoint yourself.

a. I bless my mouth. I forgive myself for . . .
(Example: the harsh words I spoke to my employee)

_____

_____

_____

b. I bless my hands. I forgive myself for. . .

_____

_____

_____

c.   I bless my _____. I forgive myself for. . .

_____

_____

_____

d.   I bless my _____. I forgive myself for. . .

_____

_____

_____

_____

6.   Record your thoughts and feelings after one of these cleansings.

_____

_____

_____

_____

_____

_____

ACTIVITY 4.4
SELF-ESTEEM QUOTATIONS

Note To The Leader

As discussed in Chapter 6 of *Enhancing Self-Esteem*, several different issues are to be considered in the maintenance phase. Review this section of Chapter 6.

Background Information

Some issues in life are of greater significance than others to some individuals. For example, some people might have greater difficulty with risk taking in this phase than with goal setting.

Purpose

To help you focus on specific issues of importance in maintaining self-esteem.

Time Required

Approximately 20 to 30 minutes

Participants

Middle school children through adults in an individual or a group setting

Materials Needed

Signs, posters, or 3" x 5" cards with the following self-esteem quotations. (Additional self-esteem quotations of your choosing could also be used.)

Procedure

1. Ask each participant to read the list of quotations being mindful of which quotations especially seem relevant to his or her problem area(s) in maintaining self-esteem. In a group setting an often helpful procedure is to play New Age music of a contemplative nature or other instrumental music which encourages introspection while each person reviews these quotations.

2. Choose one or two quotations which embody an area of self-esteem which you want to improve.

3. Write a goal according to the guidelines in Self-Esteem Goal Setting for each quotation chosen.

4. Publicly state your goal so as to enable you to become more fully committed to the goal.

5. Review your progress towards this goal daily or weekly.

> *The thing that keeps people from becoming enlightened is that they believe they don't deserve it.*

When a man no longer confuses himself with the definition of himself that others have given him, he is at once universal and unique.

We must all earn the right to be loved and do not expect love if you are incapable of giving it. Ano Ano, Kristin Zambucka

Our present experience is the result of past decisions . . . Change your mind today and you build your world of tomorrow. Your mind is your garden. . .tend it well. Ano Ano, Kristen Zambucka

The greatest gift one can give to another is the activation of the potential for positive self-esteem. Diane Frey

After you understand all about the sun and the stars and rotation of the earth, you may still miss the radiance of the sunset. Alfred North Whitehead

Most people are just about as happy as they make up their minds to be. Mark Twain

Man is the only animal that laughs and weeps; for man is the only animal that perceives how things are and how they ought to be. William Hazlitt

The mind is like a parachute. It only works when it is open. Robbie Katz

A fault recognized is half corrected. Old Proverb

You can tell more about a person by what he says about others than you can by what others say about him. Marvin Gregory

Following the path of least resistance is what makes men and rivers crooked. Voltaire

A child seldom gives the wrong answers, he just answers a different question. Anonymous

Look forward to the butterfly instead of stepping on the caterpillar. Eleanor Wynne

In all things, we learn only from those we love. Goethe

Until I accept my faults, I will most certainly doubt my virtues. Hugh Prather

Perhaps the most important single course of a person's success or failure educationally has to do with the question of what he believes about himself. Arthur Combs

Oliver Wendell Holmes once attended a meeting in which he was the shortest man present. "Doctor Holmes," quipped a friend, "I should think you'd feel rather small among us big fellows." "I do," retorted Holmes, "I feel like a dime among a lot of pennies."

The child must first learn self-respect and a sense of dignity that grows out of his increasing self-understanding before he can learn to respect the personalities and rights and differences of others. Virginia Axline

If facts are the seeds that later produce knowledge and wisdom, then the emotions and the impressions of the senses are the fertile soil in which the seeds must grow. Rachael Carson

Doubts are more cruel than the worst of truths. Molie're

An optimist is wrong just about as often as a pessimist is, but the big difference is that he had a lot more fun. Anonymous

Learning is to value oneself, having high seljf-esteem, having confidence can happen to anyone despite past learnings. Virginia Satir

Everything has its beauty, but not everyone sees it. Confucious

To thine ownself be true, and it must follow as the night the day, thou canst not then be false to any man. Shakespeare

There is no value judgement more important to man—no factor more decisive in his psychological development and motivation—than the estimate he passes on himself. Branden

The self is the star in every performance. A. Combs

Each person has a desire to maximize his/her potential. In reaching potential individuals become self-actualized. Maslow

I'm not perfect but. . . parts of me are excellent. Diane Frey

An individual rarely exceeds his/her expectations. Anonymous

Each of us is a sculptor with the power and ability to shape our own life. Anonymous

While self-esteem has some basic form, it can primarily be seen as a process of development which occurs over a lifetime. Diane Frey

Improvement is one aspect of self-esteem, even if it is peripheral. . .often is the catalyst for future changes. Diane Frey

Whether you think you can or think you can't, you're right. Henry Ford

Time is not the relevant factor in change, awareness is . . . Time only provides the opportunity. Satir

Like a gardener who plants seeds, each new look at oneself is a seed. The gardener must plant many seeds to produce a few plants. Keep at it. Diane Frey

Children have more need of models than critics. Joubert

Changing self-esteem requires perseverance. The gardener patiently waits for the seed to sprout, providing moisture, light and rich soil for growth to occur. Diane Frey

Know thyself. Greek Quotation

Love thy neighbor as thyself. Matthew 22:39

ACTIVITY 4.5
SELF-ESTEEM BAGS

Background Information

This technique helps participants to focus on an awareness of how they experience themselves now and how they would like to experience themselves in the future. A focus on where one wants to be in the future helps one to maintain self-esteem over time.

Purposes

1. To increase your awareness of how you experience yourself.

2. To increase your awareness of how you would like to experience yourself in the future.

Time Required

45 minutes

Participants

Children or adults in an individual or a group setting

Materials Needed

Paper lunch bags, scissors, glue, colorful magazines, crayons

Procedure

1. Take a bag and on the outside of the bag create a montage using magazine pictures, glue, crayons and scissors. The outside of the bag should express how you currently view yourself.

2. On the inside of the bag, express in a montage how you want to experience yourself ten years from now.

3. When finished, share the outside and inside of the bag. In a group or individual counseling session, others may not add items to the outside and/or inside of the bag.

4. Record how you feel after having shared your present and future view of self.

_____

_____

_____

_____

_____

_____

ACTIVITY 4.6
SIGNIFICANT SLOGANS

Note To The Leader

Review goal setting and risk taking in Chapter 6, *Enhancing Self Esteem.*

Background Information

In this technique participants are asked to reflect on symbols of where they currently are and where they would like to be relative to self-esteem.

Purpose

To combine elements of goal setting and risk taking relative to self-esteem.

Participants

Junior high school to older adults in an individual or a group setting

Materials Needed

Paper and pencil or pen

Procedure

1. Write three famous slogans, sayings, or lines of poetry which seem appropriate to describe your life. For example: "Do unto others as you would have them do unto you," or "To err is human, but when the eraser wears out ahead of the pencil, you're overdoing it."

   _____

   _____

   _____

   _____

   _____

2. Share your three slogans with others.

3. Think of slogans which you would like to symbolize yourself in ten to fifteen years. For example: "I've had a lot of trouble in my life, much of which never happened." Mark Twain

   _____

   _____

   _____

   _____

   _____

4. Share these three slogans with others and discuss what barriers you might encounter as you attempt to achieve these slogans.

5. Identify risks which might be required.

6. Choose one slogan and construct an affirmation. If the book *Enhancing Self Esteem* is available, guidelines are in Chapter 6 to assist in the achievement of this goal.

ACTIVITY 4.7
GOALS, BARRIERS, AND ACTIONS

Note To The Leader

Review Chapter 6 on goal setting.

Background Information

Maintaining self-esteem over time requires goal setting. Often barriers, real or perceived, can obstruct the achievement of these goals.

Purpose

To assist in developing goals, assessing barriers to the goal, and establishing an action plan.

Time Required

Varies as per stated goal

Participants

Middle school children to older adults in an individual or a group setting

Materials Needed

Paper, pencil or pens

Procedure

1. Write several personal self-esteem goals for the next five years.

   _____

   _____

   _____

   _____

   _____

   _____

   _____

2. Reflect on the following criteria:

   a. Are these goals their own or goals set for someone else? Cross out those that are not your own.

   b. Are the goals realistic and attainable? Cross out those goals which are impossible right now.

c. Are the goals stated positively? (A section on affirmations is in Chapter 6 of the book *Enhancing Self Esteem*.) Rephrase your goals into positive statements if they are not presently so stated.

d. Are the goals controllable by you? If the goals involve another person(s), ask them if they want to be involved. If they decline, cross out these goals.

e. Are your goals growth facilitating? If some goals are destructive to you, others or society, cross out those goals.

f. Are you willing to begin working on these goals now? If no, cross out these goals.

3. Select one to three goals from the remaining list to develop more fully and star each one selected.

4. Of those remaining goals, determine if each goal is specific—includes who, where, when, what, why, and how. Determine if the goal(s) is consistent with your belief system and values.

5. If the goal is not congruent with values, either cross it off the list or modify it.

6. Write the remaining or modified goal in the following space.

_____

_____

_____

_____

_____

_____

_____

_____

_____

7. List what you are willing to give up to achieve the goal.

_____

_____

_____

_____

_____

_____

8. Identify barriers to achieving the goal.

_____
_____
_____
_____
_____

9. Identify possible solutions for over coming these barriers.

_____
_____
_____
_____
_____

10. List other actions you would be willing to take to achieve the goal.

_____
_____
_____
_____
_____

11. Specify what encouragement(s) you will give yourself and/or expect from others in order for you to continue your efforts. (Self-talk technique may be helpful.)

_____
_____
_____
_____
_____

12. Review periodically (daily or weekly) to check for the progress and keep a summarized record so that you can mentally process the progress.

ACTIVITY 4.8
IN TWENTY-FIVE WORDS OR LESS...

Purpose

To assist you in focusing on advice which will help you to continue to develop and sustain self-esteem in the maintenance phase of enhancing self-esteem.

Time Required

20 to 30 minutes

Participants

Children in third grade to older adults in an individual or a group setting

Materials Needed

3" x 5" index cards, pens, pencils, and/or crayons

Procedure

1. On a 3" x 5" index card write in twenty-five words or less your best advice for enhancing self-esteem.

2. If in a group setting, collect all the cards and have each person to choose a card and read the "words of wisdom."

3. Choose the advice you like best from the group and write it in the following space.

_____

_____

_____

_____

_____

4. Read your chosen advice (Item 3) at least once a day, and act on the advice daily.

Variations in Procedure

1. Have the facilitator collect all the cards (if conducting a self-esteem group), type everyone's suggestions, duplicate the list, and distribute it to everyone on a "Primer on Self-Esteem Enhancement."

2. If the facilitator is working in an individual setting have the client periodically to write a twenty-five words or less card and accumulate a pile of such cards for review and continued focus on enhancing self-esteem.

ACTIVITY 4.9
SELF-ESTEEM CHECKLIST

Note To The Leader

Review Chapter 6 in *Enhancing Self Esteem* for a thorough discussion of symptoms of low self-esteem.

Background Information

As an introduction to the first phase of intervention, a checklist of symptoms of low self-esteem is often helpful in developing insight about the degree of involvement in low self-esteem.

Purposes

1. To have you review symptoms of low self-esteem.

2. To have you identify which low self-esteem symptoms are applicable to yourself.

3. To have you consider ways to improve your low self-esteem behaviors.

Time Required

20 to 30 minutes

Participants

Middle school age children to older adults

Materials Needed

Checklist and pencils or pens

Procedure

1. Read the following checklist and complete it for yourself. The brief checklist gives an idea of the problem area(s) for intervening and thus enhancing self-esteem. (Not all people with low self-esteem have the same symptom areas.)

Self-Esteem Checklist

		Almost Always	Often	Rarely	Never
a.	Do you brag or exaggerate your behavior?	___	___	___	___
b.	Are you jealous of others?	___	___	___	___

	Almost Always	Often	Rarely	Never
c. Do you compare yourself to others?	___	___	___	___
d. Are you possessive in your relationships with others?	___	___	___	___
e. Is it difficult for you to admit your mistakes?	___	___	___	___
f. Do you "put down" others in order to feel better yourself?	___	___	___	___
g. Are you perfectionistic?	___	___	___	___
h. Are you fearful of new experiences?	___	___	___	___
i. Are you uncomfortable when receiving compliments?	___	___	___	___
j. Are you reluctant to express your feelings and opinions?	___	___	___	___
k. Are you more concerned with meeting the needs of others rather than meeting your needs?	___	___	___	___
l. Are you reluctant to take responsibility for various life tasks?	___	___	___	___

2. Consider "Almost Always" or "Often" answers to any of these questions as symptoms that may need improvement so as to enhance your self-esteem.

3. Choose one of the items from the check list on which to improve. The one chosen is

_____.

4. Identify realistic steps you will use to improve the behavior listed in Item 3.

_____

_____

_____

ACTIVITY 4.10
BUTTON, BUTTON,
WHO'S GOT THE BUTTON?

Note To The Leader

These self estimates, as discussed in Chapter 1 of *Enhancing Self Esteem,* represent perceived weaknesses and/or unstable self. Review this section in Chapter 1 and the section on filtering feedback in Chapter 6.

Background Information

Everyone seems to have areas of psychological vulnerability.

Purpose

To help identify areas within yourself in which you can filter feedback more effectively.

Time Required

Approximately 20 minutes

Participants

High school students and/or adults in an individual or a group setting

Materials Needed

Paper and pencil

Procedure

1. Choose a time when interruptions are not likely to occur.

2. Think about various types of feedback you have been given about yourself.

3. Identify what type of feedback seems to be the most hurtful.

   _____

   _____

   _____

   _____

4. Write the most hurtful types of feedback.

   _____

   _____

   _____

   _____

5. Use the Self Mandala and ascertain what area of self these statements (Items 2, 3, and 4) seem to represent. These feedback statements represent one's "freaky buttons" or points of vulnerability.

6. Ask yourself, "Who has the button? You or others?"

7. Identify what you can do to improve these areas of self and to filter feedback more effectively in these areas?

_____

_____

_____

ACTIVITY 4.11
WALLET IDENTIFICATION

Background Information

Often participants can share information about themselves symbolically in a less threatening way through the use of familiar objects around them.

Purpose

To share some of yourself through use of objects meaningful to you.

Time Required

Approximately 10 minutes

Participants

Middle school children or older in an individual or a group setting

Material Needed

The wallet of each participant

Procedure

1. Choose an item from their wallet which represents your personal or professional characteristics or skills.

2. Share the item chosen and explain why the object is representative of your skill or traits.

ACTIVITY 4.12
THE THREE R'S
(Reading, Writing, and Rithmetic)

Background Information

This activity helps individuals to understand their identity through symbolic representation.

Purpose

To help you better understand your identity.

Time Required

Approximately 15 to 20 minutes

Participants

Children and adults in individual or group settings

Materials Needed

Pencil and paper for each participant

Procedure

1. Write "Reading, Writing, and 'Rithmetic" at the top of a sheet of paper.

2. Under "Reading" write the title of a book which might describe you.

3. Under "Writing" write a letter which describes you.

4. Under " 'Rithmetic" write your favorite number.

5. Share these symbols and tell why the book describes you.

6. Help others understand how the letter is special to you.

7. Help others understand why the chosen number is special to you.

ACTIVITY 4.13
WORDS OF LOVE FROM THE HEART

Background Information

For some people verbalizing positive feedback is very difficult. Another way to offer this feedback is through the use of written feedback. The use of written feedback cards makes it easier to begin the process of positive feedback and also involves all three major learning modalities—visual, auditory, and kinesthetic.

Purpose

To enable you to give positive feedback to others.

Time Required

25 minutes

Participants

Children and adults in individual and group setting

Procedure

1. If available, but not essential, review a set of cards called *Words of Love From the Heart,* which have been developed to facilitate giving and receiving positive feedback. Such cards say things such as, "I am so lucky to have you for a friend." or "I believe in you. I know you can do it." or "I really admire how you set goals and follow them." Such cards could also be made by a group of children and adults for exchanges in their group, their school, their work, and/or their home.

2. Acquire some blank index cards.

3. Write a comment on each card that you would like to tell someone else. You also could put drawings on the card.

4. Deliver or mail your card to the special person.

5. Make several different cards to deliver each week.

NOTE: For further information about *Words of Love From the Heart,* write to Lucia Hooker, 1528 W. Lynn Drive, Beavercreek, Ohio 45432.

ACTIVITY 4.14
SELF-ESTEEM AFFIRMATIONS

Note To The Leader

In *Enhancing Self Esteem* on pages 133-134, several guidelines are given for constructing affirmations.

Background Information

The statements in this activity represent examples of several affirmations which can be used to enhance self-esteem. The concept from which the affirmation has been constructed is stated first, followed by the affirmation. Knowing the guidelines (obtain from your leader) for affirmations, one can state very specific, explicit goals for self-improvement.

Purpose

To state specific, explicit goals for self-improvement.

Time Required

Affirmations should be done at least three times a day. As in learning any new skill, practice is necessary for affirmations to become fully realized in ones life.

Participants

Middle school students through adults (Young children can also do affirmations. Use the guidelines in *Enhancing Self Esteem* to assist in stating them in appropriate form and in suitable vocabulary.)

Materials Needed

3" x 5" cards with affirmations written on them and pens or pencils

Procedure

1. Review the affirmation cards and choose two or three which seem relevant to your self-esteem needs for improvement.

2. Read the card and try to involve as many senses as possible while visualizing the behavior desired.

3. Practice saying the affirmation at least three times a day.

4. Write affirmations of your own. For example, if you have difficulty accepting compliments, you could write, "I am calmly accepting compliments." Practice these also.

"The greatest gift one can give is the activation of the potential for positive self-esteem." Diane Frey — — — — — — — — — — I am enthusiastically activating my and others potential for positive self-esteem today and everyday of my life.	*"There is no value-judgment more important to man—no factor more decisive in his psychological development and motivation—than the estimate he passes on himself."* N. Branden — — — — — — — — — — I am lovingly choosing to judge myself in positive ways.
Just by reading this card I have decided to affirm myself and that is a good decision. — — — — — — — — — — I am enthusiastically and thoughtfully reading and visualizing my affirmation daily.	*"Whether you find you can or you think you can't, you're right."* Henry Ford — — — — — — — — — — I am enjoying knowing that I can.
An individual rarely exceeds his/her expectations. Anonymous — — — — — — — — — I am proudly and confidently setting high expectations for myself.	*When you give what has meaning for you from the heart, the receiver receives not only the gift, but a portion of your heart and therein is the value.* Anonymous — — — — — — — — — — I am joyfully giving from my heart.
"To thine ownself be true, and it must follow as the night the day, thou canst not then be false to any man." Shakespeare — — — — — — — — — — I am proudly and joyfully being true to myself more and more each day of my life.	*"Know thyself."* Greek quotation — — — — — — — — — — I am enjoying knowing myself more and more everyday.

"Everything has its beauty but not everyone sees it." Confucius

— — — — — — — — — —

I am joyfully seeing the beauty in myself and others, today and everyday of my life!

"The self is the star of every performance." A. Combs

— — — — — — — — — —

I am confidently "starring" in everything I say or do!

"Improvement in one aspect of self-esteem even if peripheral. . . often is the catalyst for future changes." Frey and Carlock

— — — — — — — — — —

I am enjoying improving an aspect of myself.

"You see things and you say 'why?' but I dream things that never were; and I say, 'why not?'" G.B. Shaw

— — — — — — — — — —

I am enthusiastically living my dream everyday.

"I'm not perfect but - - - parts of me are excellent." Frey and Carlock

— — — — — — — — — —

I am proudly celebrating the parts of me that are excellent!

"Learning to value oneself, having high self-esteem, having confidence can happen to anyone despite past learnings." Virginia Satir

— — — — — — — — — —

I am easily learning to value myself more and more each day.

"Like a gardener who plants seeds, each new look at oneself is a seed. The gardener must plant many seeds to produce a few plants. Keep at it." Frey and Carlock

— — — — — — — — — —

I am confidently and patiently planting the seeds of positive self-esteem as I read and reread my affirmations.

"Changing self-esteem requires perseverance. The gardener patiently waits for the seed to sprout, providing moisture, light and rich soil for growth to occur." Frey and Carlock

— — — — — — — — — —

I am patiently preserving in my effort to enhance my self-esteem.

"Time is not the relevant factor in change, awareness is. . . Time only provides the opportunity." V. Satir	*"Change in self-concept may occur at any time."* V. Satir
— — — — — — — — —	— — — — — — — — —
I am enthusiastically increasing my awareness.	I am enjoying the positive changes I see in myself daily.

ACTIVITY 4.15
SELF-ESTEEM GOAL SETTING

Background Information

Without a clear vision of what one wants in life with regard to self-esteem, one has difficulty in achieving self improvement goals. It is much like being blindfolded and trying to throw a dart at a target. Difficulty in accomplishing the goal is too mildly stated. Unachieveable is more appropriate if one cannot see the target (the goal). The more clearly defined a goal is, the more likely it is to be accomplished.

Purpose

To enable you to set goals effectively. Thereby gaining a sense of accomplishment which will enhance self-esteem.

Time Required

20 minutes

Participants

Children and/or adults in an individual and a group setting

Materials Needed

3" x 5" cards, pencils and pens

Procedure

1. Review the "Guidelines for Goal Setting."

2. Write a self-esteem goal for yourself using these guidelines.

   _____

   _____

   _____

   _____

   _____

3. Visualize yourself involved in the goal, and experience yourself doing the goal. (The more senses you can involve in the goal setting process, the better.)

   _____

   _____

   _____

   _____

4. Practice visualizing yourself having accomplished the goal at least once a day.

5. Every three days, write a statement about how you feel as a result of your "visualization practice."

    a.   Three days afterwards

_____

_____

_____

_____

_____

    b.   Six days afterwards

_____

_____

_____

_____

_____

    c.   Nine days afterwards

_____

_____

_____

_____

_____

Guidelines for Goal Setting*

1. The goal should be **conceivable.** The person should be able to understand the goal and identify what might be a first step.

2. Each goal should be **believable.** The person should believe that she/he can accomplish the goal.

3. Goals should be **achievable.** Each goal should be accomplishable given the strengths and abilities of each individual. For example, it would not be achievable for a ten year old to set a goal of bench pressing 150 pounds.

4. Goals should be **controllable.** Goals should be stated with regard to what is in the control of each person. For example, a goal which involves being happily married to a movie star is not controllable since such a relationship requires the agreement of both parties. Goals which involve one's own behavior are controllable.

5. Goals should be **measurable** in time and quantity. A goal of being self actualized, while very positive is too nebulous. It is better to state that one wants to clean two rooms of their house by Sunday evening rather than saying s/he want to have a clean house. It is easier to tell if you have accomplished a goal if it is for a time element stated and a quantity specifically stated.

6. Every goal should be **desirable.** A goal should reflect something one wants to do rather than something one feels s/he must do.

7. Goals should be stated with **no alternatives.** Research indicates that stating a goal by saying "I'll do _____ a _____ " only leads to doing neither. This does not imply that flexibility is not upstart. If one changes a goal, one would state the new goal without an alternative.

8. Every goal should be **growth — facilitating.** Goals should not be destructive to oneself, others or society. The goal of spray painting ten cars by midnight on Saturday meets many of the prior guidelines but is not growth facilitating or helpful to the enhancement of self-esteem.

*Note: These guidelines are adopted from *Choose Success: How to Set and Achieve All Your Goals* by B. Sharp and C. Cox, 1970 and published by Hawthorn Books, New York.

ACTIVITY 4.16
WORRY BUSTER

Note To The Leader

Review pages 205-210 and pages 257-271 in *Enhancing Self Esteem* before doing this activity. Review and understand the Johari Window. The principles of it are applicable to this activity.

Background Information

This technique can be used to help individuals learn to use the criteria of control and importance to ascertain the degree to which they might worry about something.

Purpose

To understand how to manage self worry more effectively.

Time Required

45 to 60 minutes

Participants

Intermediate grade children and older and/or adults in an individual or a group setting

Materials Needed

Two pieces of notebook size paper for each person, pencils

Procedure

1. Mentally review a book you have read or obtain a book to read regarding aspects of worry and how too much worry can lead to stress which can have a negative effect on self-esteem.

2. On one piece of paper write everything you worry about, including such things as personal health, extended family, work concerns, neighborhood and community issues, life questions, global issues and trivia.

3. Recognize that worrying is a waste of energy when it motivates one to take action to deal with a perceived threat.

4. Practice worrying wisely, that is, expend energy on those issues which you can control and on those things you do value.

5. Construct a Worry Window with four panes. This Worry Window goes on the second piece of paper you need. The paper is sectioned according to the following diagram:

Pane I Important: Can Control	**Pane II** Important: Can't Control
Pane III Not Important: Can Control	**Pane IV** Not Important: Can't Control

6. Survey your list of worries and transfer each worry to the appropriate pane of the Worry Window using the following guidelines: Pane I—Write those worries that are important and are in your control. Pane II—Write those worries that are important but are not in your control. Pane III—Write those worries that are NOT important and are in your control. Pane IV—Write those worries that are NOT important and are NOT in your control. Keep in mind two important questions: Is this really important to me? Is this in my control?

7. If Pane I is very filled, reevaluate how important each worry actually is to you.

8. If Pane II is very filled, think about either gaining more control of the worry and moving it to Pane I or deciding to let the worry go.

9. If Pane III is very filled recognize that these worries are neither important, nor in one's control. It is a waste of time to worry about these. Cross them off the list. It is amazing how often people will worry about things which are not important solely because they do have control of the issue.

10. Choose an item in each pane to stop worrying about.

11. Write a goal for the worry selected in Pane I.

_____

_____

_____

_____

_____

12. Write a brief description of how the goal in Item 11 will be accomplished.

_____

_____

_____

_____

_____

13. Write a goal for the worry selected in Pane II.

_____

_____

_____

_____

_____

14. Write a brief description of how the goal in Item 13 will be accomplished.

_____

_____

_____

_____

_____

_____

CONCLUSION

CONCLUSION

"A person without goals is like a traveler without a destination." The hope is that, having completed activities in this workbook, you and those you care about can have a destination—that of positive self-esteem. Perhaps you need a new map for this destination. One different from the one you have been using. Perhaps your map needs to be your map and not the map of someone else. Perhaps you need to pave over old ruts in your road and/or create new pathways.

Regardless of your situation, remember you are in the driver's seat. You are in control of the development of your self-esteem. In the travel you can easily get discouraged. Reaching an improved self-esteem destination requires patience and perseverance. You need to be willing to put up with the pain of road construction. The journey is not necessarily easy, but arriving at the destination makes the journey well worth it.

Best wishes for your journey and the journeys of those you help.

DIANE E. FREY

Dr. Frey earned her Ph.D. in counseling from the University of Illinois and is currently Professor of Counseling at Wright State University, Dayton, Ohio.

In addition to her teaching and writing, she maintains a private practice as a licensed clinical psychologist in Dayton, Ohio. Dr. Frey conducts seminars on self-esteem, stress management, conflict management, the emotional needs of the gifted, and other personal growth topics for educational, business, and industrial clients. She has been guest lecturer at Indiana University and Purdue University. Dr. Frey has served as visiting professor of clinical psychology at the Hawaii School of Professional Psychology and the Forest Institute of Professional Psychology.

An internationally known speaker, Dr. Frey has appeared as a guest on talk shows in Hawaii, California, Ohio, and Indiana, as well as serving as keynote speaker and/or major presenter for the World Conference on the Gifted and Talented, The International Conference for Play Therapy, the National Conference on Supporting the Emotional Needs of the Gifted, the American Association for Counseling and Development, the American Psychological Association (APA), MENSA, and numerous state and regional conferences.

Dr. Frey has recently authored the book, *Intimate Relationships.* She is on the editorial boards of the *Elementary School Guidance and Counseling Journal* and the *Journal of Counseling Psychology.* In addition, she is on the Board of Directors of the National Council for Self Esteem. Dr. Frey is also a member of the National Accreditation Board of APA and a board member of the Neuro Linguistic Programming Foundation.

C. JESSE CARLOCK

Dr. C. Jesse Carlock earned her Ph.D. at the Florida State University in Tallahassee, Florida. Working with individuals, groups, couples, and families, she has been a psychologist in private practice for the past 12 years. Dr. Carlock specializes in work with those recovering from addictions, eating disorders, adult children of dysfunctional families, and survivors of childhood trauma. Currently, she is Clinical Associate Professor with the School of Professional Psychology at Wright State University. She is also a trainer with the Gestalt Institute of Southern Ohio and Virginia Satir's Avanta Network.

Dr. Carlock is also co-director of Peoplemaking Midwest, an organization which offers workshops, training, consultation, and publications in Virginia Satir's model of self-esteem enhancement. She has written numerous articles in the areas of group work, couples therapy, alcoholism, and adult children of alcoholics.